Second Stitches

Recycle as You Sew

Other books available from Chilton ▶

Robbie Fanning, Series Editor

Contemporary Quilting Series

Appliqué the Ann Boyce Way
  by Ann Boyce
Contemporary Quilting Techniques
  by Pat Cairns
Fast Patch
  by Anita Hallock
Fourteen Easy Baby Quilts
  by Margaret Dittman
*Machine-Quilted Jackets, Vests, and
  Coats*
  by Nancy Moore
Pictorial Quilts
  by Carolyn Vosburg Hall
*Precision Pieced Quilts Using the
  Foundation Method*
  by Jane Hall and Dixie Haywood
The Quilter's Guide to Rotary Cutting
  by Donna Poster
Quilts by the Slice
  by Beckie Olson
Scrap Quilts Using Fast Patch
  by Anita Hallock
Speed-Cut Quilts
  by Donna Poster
Super Simple Quilts
  by Kathleen Eaton
*Teach Yourself Machine Piecing and
  Quilting*
  by Debra Wagner
Three-Dimensional Appliqué
  by Jodie Davis

Craft Kaleidoscope Series

Fabric Painting Made Easy
  by Nancy Ward
How to Make Cloth Books for Children
  by Anne Pellowski

Star Wear Series

Sweatshirts with Style,
  by Mary Mulari

Creative Machine Arts Series

ABCs of Serging
  by Tammy Young and Lori Bottom
The Button Lover's Book
  by Marilyn Green
Claire Shaeffer's Fabric Sewing Guide
*The Complete Book of Machine
  Embroidery*
  by Robbie and Tony Fanning
Creative Nurseries Illustrated
  by Debra Terry and Juli Plooster
Creative Serging Illustrated
  by Pati Palmer, Gail Brown, and
  Sue Green
Distinctive Serger Gifts and Crafts
  by Naomi Baker and Tammy Young
The Fabric Lover's Scrapbook
  by Margaret Dittman
Friendship Quilts by Hand and Machine
  by Carolyn Vosburg Hall
Gifts Galore
  by Jane Warnick and Jackie Dodson
How to Make Soft Jewelry
  by Jackie Dodson
Innovative Serging
  by Gail Brown and Tammy Young
Innovative Sewing
  by Gail Brown and Tammy Young
*Owner's Guide to Sewing Machines,
  Sergers, and Knitting Machines*
  by Gale Grigg Hazen
Petite Pizzazz
  by Barb Griffin
Putting on the Glitz
  by Sandra L. Hatch and Ann Boyce
Serged Garments in Minutes
  by Tammy Young and Naomi Baker
Sew Sensational Gifts
  by Naomi Baker and Tammy Young
Sew, Serge, Press
  by Jan Saunders
Sewing and Collecting Vintage Fashions
  by Eileen MacIntosh
Simply Serge Any Fabric
  by Naomi Baker and Tammy Young
*Soft Gardens: Make Flowers with Your
  Sewing Machine*
  by Yvonne Perez-Collins
Twenty Easy Machine-Made Rugs
  by Jackie Dodson

Know Your Sewing Machine Series
by Jackie Dodson

Know Your Bernina, second edition
Know Your Brother
  with Jane Warnick
Know Your Elna
  with Carol Ahles
Know Your New Home
  with Judi Cull and Vicki Lyn
  Hastings
Know Your Pfaff
  with Audrey Griese
Know Your Sewing Machine
Know Your Singer
Know Your Viking
  with Jan Saunders
Know Your White
  with Jan Saunders

Know Your Serger Series
by Tammy Young and Naomi Baker

Know Your baby lock
Know Your Pfaff Hobbylock
Know Your Serger
Know Your White Superlock

Teach Yourself to Sew Better Series
by Jan Saunders

A Step-by-Step Guide to Your Bernina
*A Step-by-Step Guide to Your New
  Home*
*A Step-by-Step Guide to Your Sewing
  Machine*
A Step-by-Step Guide to Your Viking

Susan D. Parker

Second Stitches

Recycle as You Sew

Chilton Book Company

Radnor, Pennsylvania

Photography by Nancy Clevinger and Ben and Patricia Simmons

Illustrations by the author

Book design by Arlene Putterman

Border design from Cliptures™ by Dream Maker Software®.
© 1992 Dream Maker Software. All rights reserved.

Manufactured in the United States of America.

Library of Congress Cataloging-in-Publication Data
Parker, Susan D. (Susan Denise), 1953–
    Second stitches : recycle as you sew / Susan D. Parker.
      p. cm.—(Creative machine arts)
    Includes index.
    ISBN 0-8019-8476-9
    1. Sewing. 2. Clothing and dress—Remaking. I. Title.
  II. Series: Creative machine arts series.
TT715.P37   1993
646.2—dc20   93-27478
                                     CIP

3 4 5 6 7 8 9 0   2 1 0 9 8 7 6 5

*Are you interested in a quarterly newsletter about creative uses
of the sewing machine, serger, and knitting machine?
Write to The Creative Machine, PO Box 2634, Menlo Park, CA 94026.*

To Daddy,
who always thought I could

Contents

Foreword

THINK about the things you throw away every day. Has your awareness of discarded items risen with the national publicity to save Mother Earth? I know I've consciously resisted wastefulness as I've patched a quilt, composted vegetable peelings, or recovered a chair—all in a pragmatic effort to increase my residential responsibility. Yet I've often found myself throwing out beautiful fabric and buttons just because they seemed out of date. I wanted to recycle them, but I had no real project in mind, so I let them go.

How pleased I am that Susan Parker has come to my rescue (and yours) and organized choice creative ideas for recycled fabric. Not only does Susan provide numerous ways to make use of an overflowing fabric stash, she also offers suggestions for reusing sewing notions and little-used accessories and clothing. Best of all, Susan has arranged the processes of "what" and "how" in a creative, easy-to-use reference. Redo! Rethink! Resew! Resave! Susan shows us the way. It is tempting to try a recycling blitz and attempt all of her suggestions, but if reality settles in and you approach only one or two projects, you'll find it a snap to follow each chapter's precise, simple format. Each of Susan's chapters outlines one recycling topic, such as rescaling clothing, creative uses for remnants—even making cloth bags. My favorite is her chapter of 25 quick recycling hints.

Now almost everything can be better the second time around. From page one to the end, Susan offers multiple choices for those of us who enjoy the challenge of making something out of nothing: from the necessity of a baby's burp cloth to the cleverness of button jewelry. Susan is especially innovative with her approach to second-time-around garments, sharing great hints on embellishment and refurbishing. Adding decorative stitching to an odd-colored belt so that it coordinates with an existing outfit, brightening up an old vest with a random display of buttons, and using old jeans to create everything from a change purse to a bathrobe are just some of Susan's innovations.

Now we can seriously challenge ourselves to look twice before tossing anything again. Finally, it is logical to enforce "less is more" and make a true effort to extend the stash around us a second or even third time around. Susan's efforts put her talents first-step forward—and encourage us to do the same.

Alice Allen
Sewing author and educator

Acknowledgments

My thanks to:

▶ Bernina of America, Inc., for the continuing information and education they provide.

▶ Charlou Lunsford for all of her help in sewing samples and checking details.

▶ Alice Allen for her inspiration and her friendship.

▶ Ben and Patricia Simmons of Simmons Photography for their wonderful help and their beautiful photographs.

▶ Robbie Fanning and the Chilton Book Company for their patience in working with a first-time author.

Introduction
The Importance of Recycling

AS A CHILD, I was fascinated by new things. Shopping malls were just beginning to spring up, and the world seemed full of an endless array of gadgets, garments, and good things to buy. What I didn't realize then, as most people didn't, was that the world was also generating an amazing amount of garbage. As we became a disposable society, we gave little, if any, thought to where those disposables went. Only in the last few years, as our landfills have become full and the garbage has begun to pile up, have we started to look for ways to conserve our natural resources and help save our planet.

We now know that we can't continue with the mindless disposal of anything we choose. The amount of garbage thrown away in the United States is equal to 3½ to 4 pounds per person *per day*! We throw away clothes, food, furniture, cars, appliances, and all types of reusable objects without a second thought. Our aim is to get it out of sight so that we don't have to think about it anymore. The trouble is, *someone* has to think about it. The majority of the things that we throw away today will still be on this earth in our great-grandchildren's time. In fact, many of the items that we discard will *never* decompose. They will be here taking up space as long as the earth is here. That is why we must start now to reduce what we use, recycle as much as possible, and reuse things whenever we have the opportunity to do so.

As we've become aware of the trash situation over the last decade, many of us have started doing our part by recycling paper and aluminum

1

cans and paying attention to how we use materials on a daily basis. We've been aided in our efforts by scores of books written to help everyone from schoolchildren to office managers learn how to recycle. However, this massive educational effort seems to have overlooked one of the most likely candidates for recycling: the stitcher. Many of us began sewing in an effort to save money and make the most of limited resources, so it seems only natural that we would look for ways to recycle fabrics, notions, and supplies.

Recycling and reusing all sorts of items also takes advantage of a sewer's creativity. Designing new solutions to the daily recycling situations found in the sewing room requires a great deal of imagination and resourcefulness—qualities that sewers use every day.

Much of this book deals with sewing projects that use up the extra fabric, notions, and other supplies that all of us have stashed in our sewing area. But recycling for sewers doesn't stop there. With our special skills and ingenuity, we can also refurbish worn clothing and create reusable cloth alternatives to everyday disposable items such as shopping bags and diapers. More important, learning to recycle can give the sewer a new outlook. It becomes a challenge to use up fabric and notions completely—sometimes in ways we never dreamed of!

In the sewing room, as elsewhere, recycling includes a wide variety of activities; the possibilities available to sewers are limitless. After reading Chapter 1, "Reuse and Conserve," you'll begin to see how easy and how useful recycling in the sewing room can be. Browse through the other chapters to find projects that apply to your particular variety of "recyclables." Do you want to create cloth bags to encourage everyday recycling? Read Chapter 2. Is your button box filled to overflowing? See Chapter 8. How about those clothes earmarked as hand-me-downs or for charity collections? Chapters 1, 3, 6, and 9 may provide you with some ideas for giving these garments a second life. You can even refer to the List of Recycled Items in the back of the book to see if anything you're thinking of throwing away (or have been saving for years on end) can be put to use in the projects in this book.

The only limit to recycling in your sewing room is your imagination. This book is intended to be an inspiration and a starting point for your excursion into the world of recycling and reusing in the sewing room.

I'd like to hear about your "recycling while sewing" successes. Please write to me with any recycling innovations you've discovered. All ideas will be appropriately credited.

Susan Parker
P.O. Box 17724
Kansas City, MO 64134

Chapter 1
Reuse and Conserve

*25 Easy Ways to Recycle
Fabrics, Notions, and Supplies*

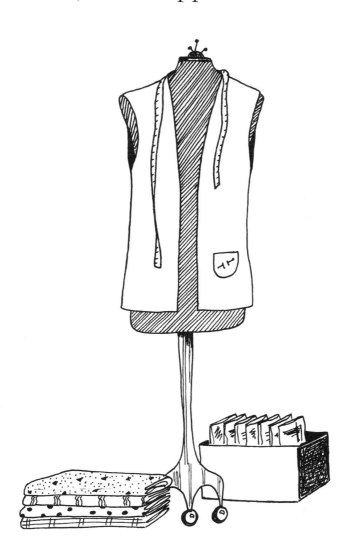

AS YOU begin to recycle, you will see situations and objects in a different light. Look around your sewing room. Use your imagination and try to think of new uses for items that in the past you would have overlooked or thrown away. It's fun to see how many projects you can sew or problems you can solve without bringing anything new into the house. In the process, you can be creative, economical, *and* reduce the amount of trash that goes to the landfills. This chapter opens up some possibilities for using and recycling what you have on hand. Use the following ideas to get started, then put your ingenuity to work on your own belongings, finding new ways to creatively reuse and recycle.

NOTIONS AND SUPPLIES

Over the last ten or fifteen years, the sewing industry has developed some wonderful notions that make sewing easier and the results more professional. It's always gratifying to find the perfect notion for the job at hand, but you may not have thought of looking around your own home or in your sewing extras to find that hidden jewel of a tool.

1 ▶ Use selvages from firmly woven prewashed fabrics (muslin, calico, silk, etc.) as a stabilizer in place of twill tape. After prewashing the fabric, check to see whether the selvages are pulled or rippled. If they are nice and flat, they are suitable to use as stabilizer tape. With a rotary cutter, trim the selvages from the fabric in needed widths (usually ¼″ [6mm] to ½″ [1.3cm]). These strips work great in shoulder seams when sewing knits, for stabilizing pocket edges, or in any place where you would usually use stabilizer tape. Store the strips in a reused plastic bag until you need them. When working with lightweight fabrics, use silk selvage strips to stabilize the garment without adding bulk.

2 ▶ Small, travel-size bars of soap can be used as marking tools on most fabrics. Use an emery board to sharpen the edge of the soap so that you get a fine line. Use the soap on washable fabrics so that you can remove the soap lines with water if necessary, although many times they can be brushed out with an old, clean toothbrush.

3 ▶ Use odd-colored zippers when making decorator throw pillows. The color of the zipper won't matter once you stitch the flap to create a hidden opening. To make a covered zippered opening on the back of the pillow, follow these simple steps: Add 1″ (2.5cm) to the width of the back of the pillow. Find the center point along the new width and split the back in half at this center point. Place the zipper face down along the right-hand center edge as shown in Figure 1-1. Straight stitch the zipper in place along the zipper tape, using a ½″ (1.3cm) seam allowance.

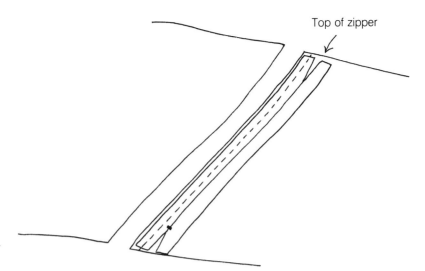

Figure 1-1
Place the zipper on the cut pillow back.

Topstitch on the right side of the fabric next to the zipper coil, if desired. Cut a 4″-wide (10cm) strip of fabric the same length as the pillow. Fold the strip in half lengthwise, right sides together, and press it. Place the folded strip at the left center edge of the pillow back, with the raw edges even. Put the unstitched side of the zipper face down on the folded strip. Stitch the zipper down with a ½″ (1.3cm) seam allowance (Fig. 1-2). Press the flap over the zipper and baste the top and bottom ends in place (Fig. 1-3). Complete the pillow according to the usual directions.

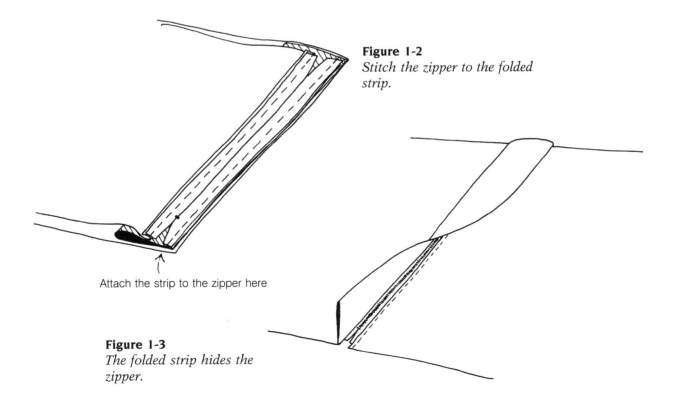

Figure 1-2
Stitch the zipper to the folded strip.

Attach the strip to the zipper here

Figure 1-3
The folded strip hides the zipper.

4 ▶ Make your own pillow forms from bonded polyester batting. Cut two pieces of batting to the desired size, adding a ½″ (1.3cm) seam allowance on all edges. Serge or zigzag stitch the two pieces together on three sides (Fig. 1-4), forming an open pocket. Stuff the pocket you've created with leftover batting, fiberfill, or scraps of pantyhose. Fabric scraps may be used, but be aware that they will usually add weight and make the

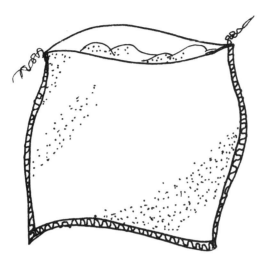

Figure 1-4
Make your own pillow forms.

pillow heavier and less fluffy than fiberfill will. If you use fabric scraps, "dice" them with a rotary cutter and mix them with scraps of batting or fleece. The batting cover will smooth out any bumps and give the pillow form an even, full look. After stuffing the form, serge or zigzag stitch the edge closed. Use the finished product as you would a purchased pillow form.

5 ▶ This great idea came from Laurie McWilliams, a designer and sewing specialist from Evansville, Indiana. She uses men's ties to create quick bias strips for bindings, pipings, and trims. The ties are already cut on the bias, so all you need to do is open the seam, flatten out the tie, and cut a strip down the middle to get a perfect piece of bias (Fig. 1-5). When selecting discarded ties for this purpose, ignore the print and the pattern of the tie fabric. All you need to consider are the colors of the tie, since the colors are all that will be visible after you cut the strips. What a great way to get rid of some not-so-great ties!

6 ▶ Another bonus to cutting strips from ties is that you get a wonderful piece of interfacing from inside the tie—just right for using in the hems of tailored jackets.

7 ▶ Save leftover pieces of ribbon and create a colorful appliqué. Place the ribbons edge to edge and fuse them to a piece of paper-backed

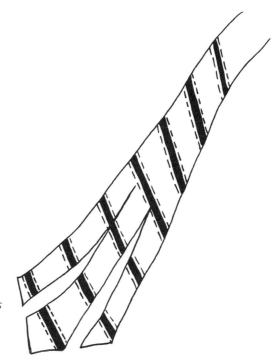

Figure 1-5
Bias strips cut from a man's tie

fusible web that is slightly larger than the appliqué shape will be (as is done with the heart appliqué shape in Fig. 1-6). After fusing the ribbons, use a medium zigzag stitch to sew them together. Using nylon thread will keep the stitching inconspicuous and allow the beauty of the ribbons to show. After creating the fabric piece, cut the appliqué shape from it. Peel off the paper backing and fuse the shape to your project. Proceed with the appliqué process.

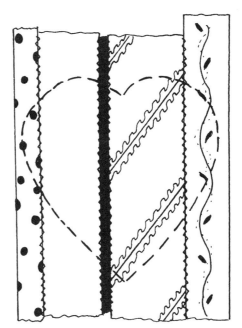

Figure 1-6
Appliqué shapes can be cut from ribbons.

8 ▶ When shopping for notions and supplies, pay attention to the packaging. Try to choose those products that have the least amount of paper and packaging to throw away. For example, buy interfacing by the yard off the bolt rather than in a plastic-wrapped package.

CLOTHING AND ACCESSORIES

Clothing can be reused and refurbished in endless ways without sacrificing style or class. Use a critical eye to examine clothes that are no longer wearable to see if you can give them a second life somehow. Also, before shopping for new fabric, pull out your fabric stash and scraps and try to picture ways to incorporate these treasures into your next clothing project.

9 ▶ Before throwing out worn garments, double-check the buttons, hooks, belt buckles, and zippers. If they are in good condition, keep them to use in future projects. Use embroidery floss to string the buttons so that they can be stored together. Thread a needle with floss, put the needle through the holes of the buttons, and tie the ends of the floss together to form a loop (Fig. 1-7). Store the buttons in a button box or hang them

Figure 1-7
*String extra buttons together
with embroidery floss.*

on a hook. After removing any thread from the zippers, spray them heavily with starch and press them flat. Sort and store the zippers by putting a safety pin through each tab and pinning the zippers onto a coat hanger.

10 ▶ Check worn-out purses for reusable frames and hardware before throwing them into the trash. The hardware usually lasts much longer than the purse and can easily be turned into a new bag. Make a pattern from the discarded purse, or purchase one of the many commercial patterns available that are designed to be used with a frame.

11 ▶ Check hand-me-downs (as well as local thrift stores and resale shops) for unusual belt buckles. You can replace the belt itself with your version of a leather, fabric, or Ultrasuede wrap and have a unique belt for a fraction of the cost. Don't overlook men's belts as possibilities for yourself. For the time it takes to make a few new holes, you can have a nice leather belt.

12 ▶ Restyle wide-leg slacks and give them a more contemporary look by taking a tuck at the lower edge (Fig. 1-8). Rip out the hem stitching and lightly press the hem flat. From the wrong side of the pants, make a

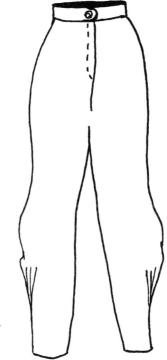

Figure 1-8
Restyle wide-leg slacks.

fold on the grain line along the side seam of the outside of each leg. Straight stitch 5″–6″ (12.5cm–15cm) up from the bottom of the leg about 2″–3″ (5cm–7.5cm) from the fold (the exact amount will depend on how wide the pant leg is and how much fabric needs to be taken out). Before stitching, check to be sure that the opening is large enough to slip your foot through. If the tuck creates too much bulk, trim away the lower portion of the seam allowance. Check the length of the pantlegs before putting the hems back in and pressing them. Often the pantleg will need to be shortened to accommodate the new styling.

13 ▶ Save small pieces of lining and blouse fabrics left over from sewing projects and use them to make pockets for other garments. When stitching in-seam pockets, simply cut the pocket pattern pieces from the lightweight fabric. The pieces will lie flat and reduce the bulk that would result from using outer-weight fabric. When making patch pockets, use the scraps as lining pieces.

14 ▶ Save larger pieces of lining to use when stitching an unconstructed jacket. Line only the sleeves to make the jacket easy to slip on and off.

15 ▶ When a favorite dress goes out of style or "out of size," recycle both its skirt and its bodice. Use the skirt to make a fashionable vest to wear with skirts, slacks, and jeans. Separate the skirt from the bodice and cut it apart at the side seams. Press the skirt fabric flat and use it to cut out the front of your favorite vest pattern. Use coordinating lining fabric as the back of the vest.

16 ▶ Use the bodice of the dress to make a dickey to wear with sweaters and jackets (Fig. 1-9). Measure 5½" (14cm) from the neck edge along the shoulder line. Cut from this point on the shoulder line down

Figure 1-9
Make a dickey from an old dress bodice.

the front and the back of the bodice to the waistline. Serge or hem the side edges, from the lower front to the lower back. Cut two pieces of ¼" (6mm) elastic, each 6"–8" (15cm–20.5cm) long, and stitch them to the front and back of the dickey at each side of the waistline. Slip the dickey over your head to wear it.

17 ▶ When lengthening a dress for a child, use a coordinating strip of fabric. Instead of tacking the strip onto the bottom of the dress or skirt, place the fabric about 4" (10cm) from the bottom, so that it becomes a part of the garment and not just an afterthought. Cut the dress or skirt all the way around, about 4" (10cm) from the bottom, and serge or stitch the strip to the cut edges of the dress. Easy, with no hemming! You could also use the new fabric in another part of the dress to pull the look together. Make a sash for the waist or a tie at the neck to give the dress a coordinated, finished look.

18 ▶ When a half-slip loses its elasticity in the waist, don't throw it out. Use the slip to line a newly made skirt. The shape of the slip should be compatible with the shape of the skirt you are making (for example, for a straight skirt, use a straight slip). Cut away the worn-out elastic on the slip and measure the length of the skirt. The slip should measure the finished length of the skirt *minus* 1″ (2.5cm) *plus* a ½″ (1.3cm) seam allowance for attaching at the waistline of the garment. Trim away any excess at the top edge of the slip to eliminate the need for rehemming. Use the slip as you would a handmade lining and attach it as you construct the waistline.

19 ▶ If a garment has a stubborn stain that will not come out, cut out the stain. Find a simple design with areas that can be cut away, such as the one shown in Figure 1-10. Position the design over the stained area

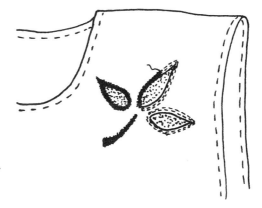

Figure 1-10
Remove a stain with cutwork.

and mark it onto the garment. Straight stitch around all the lines of the design two or three times. Depending on the weight of the fabric, you may need to place a tear-away stabilizer behind the design. Cut away portions of the design, trimming close to the stitching. Pin or baste a coordinating piece of fabric behind the design so that it shows through the cut-away areas. Using a satin stitch, stitch over the straight stitching, attaching the contrasting fabric to the garment in the process. Again, stabilizer may be needed to keep the fabric from being pulled and puckered as you sew. If you use stabilizer, pull it off after you have completed all the stitching. Trim the coordinating fabric close to the stitching on the wrong side of the garment.

GIFT WRAPPING

When wrapping gifts, save a tree by avoiding paper wrappings and using fabric instead. Many of us have fabric stashes that can provide unique choices for fabric wrappings. Making a fabric wrap is easy and usually takes no more time than shopping for paper wrapping.

20 ▶ Quickly make a personalized gift basket using a table napkin or a hemmed square of cloth. Embellish one corner of the square with fabric paint by writing the name of the recipient or any appropriate greeting. Place the cloth in a basket with the decorative corner facing front. Put your gift item(s) in the basket, tie a bow on the handle, and the gift is ready.

21 ▶ Another quick way to wrap a gift is to cut a rectangle of fabric and sew it into a gift bag. Determine the size rectangle needed for the gift. Be generous with the sizing and then cut two rectangles, one for each side of the bag. Finish the top edge of each rectangle by serging or hemming it. Place the two rectangles right sides together and serge or sew down both sides. Sew across the opening at the bottom. Turn the bag right side out and place the gift inside. Tie the bag closed with ribbon and add a bow and gift tag (Fig. 1-11).

Figure 1-11
Quick Gift-Wrap Bag

22 ▶ For larger, odd-shaped items, use a circular piece of fabric. Measure the height and width of the item and add 12″–15″ (30.5cm–38cm). This will be the radius of the circle (from the center to the edge). Fold a large piece of light- to medium-weight fabric into quarters. Measure the radius from the double-fold (center of circle) along both folded edges (Fig. 1-12). Connect these two markings with an arc and cut out the circle

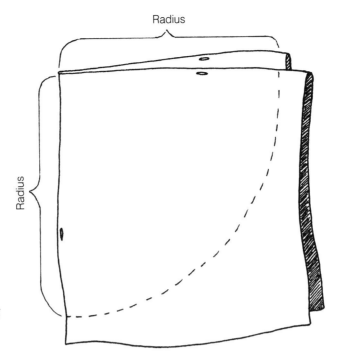

Figure 1-12
Pattern for a circle bag

along this marked line. Make a 1″ (2.5cm) slit through all the layers 1″ (2.5cm) from the fold and 10″ (25.5cm) from the outer edge of the circle (see Fig. 1-12). Open the circle. At this point, the outside edge of circle may be pinked, serged, or hemmed, if desired. Most fabrics will not require this, but you may want to do it to give your wrapping a more finished look. With the wrong side of the fabric facing up, place the gift in the center of the circle. Thread 1″ (2.5cm) of ribbon through the slits, gather up the edges around the gift, and tie the ribbon into a bow (Fig. 1-13). The best part about this wrapping is that the fabric is still usable long after the gift has been opened.

Figure 1-13
Gift wrap for larger items

AROUND THE HOUSE

When recycling, think beyond the possibilities of your sewing room. Look around your whole house to see if there are problems you can solve by recycling items that would normally be thrown away or taking up space in closets and elsewhere.

23 ▶ Covered, padded hangers help clothes retain their shape as they hang in your closet. These quick hangers are a great way to use those discarded shoulder pads that seem to multiply as fast as wire coat hangers. Select a hanger and trace around the top edge to get the shape needed for the cover (Fig. 1-14). Add ¼″ (6mm) seam allowances and ex-

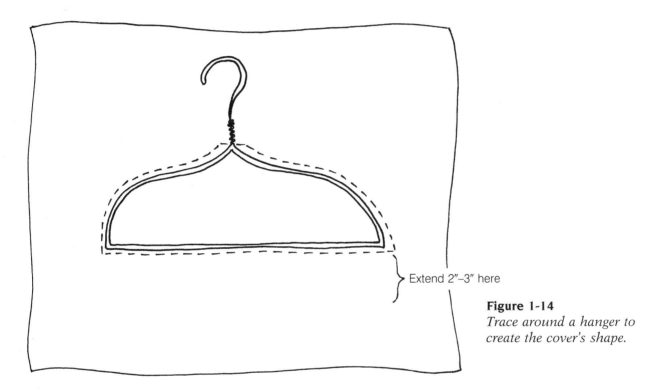

Extend 2″–3″ here

Figure 1-14
Trace around a hanger to create the cover's shape.

tend the shape down 2″–3″ (5cm–7.5cm). Using a firmly woven fabric (portions of old pillowcases and sheets work well), cut out two of the shapes and place them right sides together. Stitch along the sides and top, leaving a 2″ (5cm) opening at the center. Turn the cover right side out and serge or hem around the top center opening. Turn under the bottom edge ½″ (1.3cm) and press it. Before placing the cover on the hanger, use a pair of shoulder pads to pad the top edge. On each side of the hanger's "hook," fold at least one shoulder pad over the top edge of the hanger and tack it in place (Fig. 1-15). Slip the cover over the top of the hanger. Place the folded bottom edges together and edgestitch them closed, using a zipper foot if necessary.

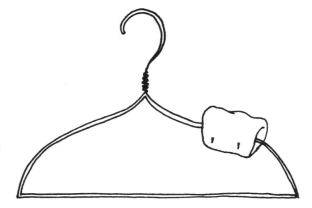

Figure 1-15
Tack each shoulder pad in place.

24 ▶ Make a hanging laundry bag that is great for small spaces. Using a large-size man's shirt, cut off the sleeves and the tail of the shirt, leaving the body of the shirt as long as possible. Turn the shirt wrong side out with the shirt buttoned and sew or serge down each side and across the bottom of the shirt. Turn the shirt right side out and place it on a hanger (Fig. 1-16). Hang the bag on the back of a door and put dirty clothes in it by unbuttoning a few of the buttons.

Figure 1-16
Hanging Clothes Hamper

25 ▶ If you've been lucky enough to have inherited your grandmother's sewing box, make an interesting centerpiece from the contents. Pour all of the buttons, notions, trims, and threads into a large, elegant glass bowl. If you need more filler, add additional colorful and interesting buttons found at flea markets and garage sales. You'll have a great conversation piece!

Chapter 2
Recycling—It's in the Bag!

*Helping the Planet Every Day
by Using Cloth Bags*

WE HAVE definitely become a society of shoppers. Shopping is no longer a necessity that we do along with our other chores. Now it is a pastime, an entertainment, and even a sport. Along with shopping comes a variety of paper and plastic bags, each one made by using up our natural resources of trees and oil. One of the least painful ways you can help save those resources is to provide your own reusable bags for your purchases. If each household in this country used its own bag for just one shopping trip, about 60,000 trees could be saved.

The following pages contain instructions for a variety of bags and sacks that are reusable and could virtually eliminate the need for paper and plastic bags. Most of these bags are made with fairly small piece of fabric, so dig through your fabric stash and look in your closets for bits and pieces left over from other projects.

▶ Sturdy Canvas Shopping Bag (Fig. 2-1)

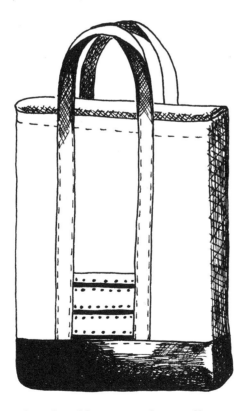

Figure 2-1
Sturdy Canvas Shopping Bag

This durable canvas bag will give you years of practical use anywhere, from the grocery store to the shoe store. With its reinforced bottom, triple-stitched handles, and handy coupon pocket, it will give you a lifetime of "environmentally friendly" service (see the Color Section).

MATERIALS NEEDED

1 yard (91.5cm) of 45″-wide (114.5cm) canvas, denim, or other sturdy fabric

2 strips of paper-backed fusible web, each 4″ × 39″ (10cm × 99cm)

DIRECTIONS

Cut the following pieces from the fabric, cutting across the grain:

- One 41″ × 16″ (104cm × 40.5cm) rectangle for the sides of the **bag**. (Mark a placement line for the reinforced base 14½″ [37cm] from each short end.)
- One 16″ × 12½″ (40.5cm × 32cm) rectangle for the **reinforced base** of the bag.
- One 5″ × 21″ (12.5cm × 53.5cm) rectangle for the **pocket**.
- Two 4″ × 39″ (10cm × 99cm) strips for the **handles**.

Using fabrics of contrasting colors and prints will make the bag even more interesting.

To make the handles, fuse the web according to the manufacturer's directions onto the wrong side of the fabric strips. Fold under ¼″ (6mm) on one long side and fuse this edge down, being careful not to touch the hot iron to the exposed web. Fold the strips into thirds, placing the raw edge to the inside (Fig. 2-2). Fuse.

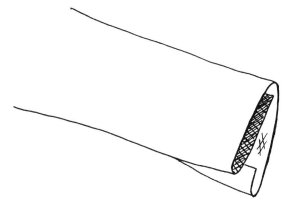

Figure 2-2
Fold the strips into thirds.

Fold ¼″ (6mm) under on the short edges of the pocket piece. Fold a second time and topstitch each edge.

Position the pocket piece on the bag by centering it side to side and top to bottom (Fig. 2-3). Baste it in place.

Position the handles on the bag with the lower edges just below the reinforced base marking (shown already stitched in Fig. 2-4). Center the handle over the side edges of the pocket.

Stitch the lower edges of the handles to the bag with a narrow zigzag stitch for strength.

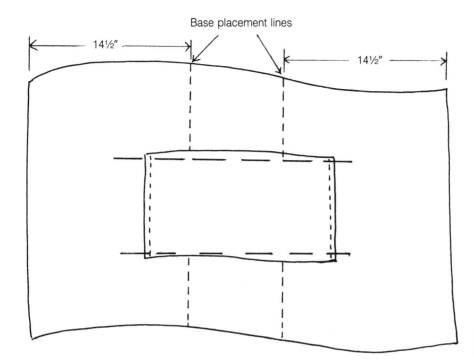

Figure 2-3
Position the pocket piece.

Edgestitch each side of the handles to the bag, stopping 1¼″ (3cm) from the raw top edge of the bag. Be sure to secure the side pocket edges with the handle stitching (see Fig. 2-4).

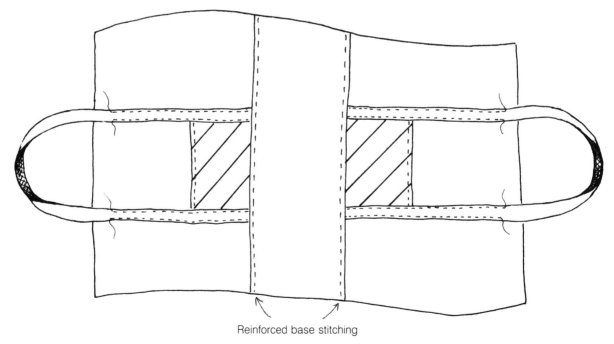

Figure 2-4
The handles, the pocket, and the reinforced base sewn into place

Fold under ¼″ (6mm) on the long sides of the base piece and press. Position the base fabric at the markings on the bag fabric, covering the lower edges of the handles.

Edgestitch along the long folded edge the base fabric, stitching across the end of the handles. If your sewing machine has a reinforced stitch (triple straight stitch), you may use this for added durability.

Fold ¼″ (6mm) under on each end of the bag and press. Fold the bag in half with right sides together. Stitch the side seams, using a ½″ (1.3cm) seam allowance (Fig. 2-5). Use a serger stitch or a narrow zigzag stitch to finish for added strength.

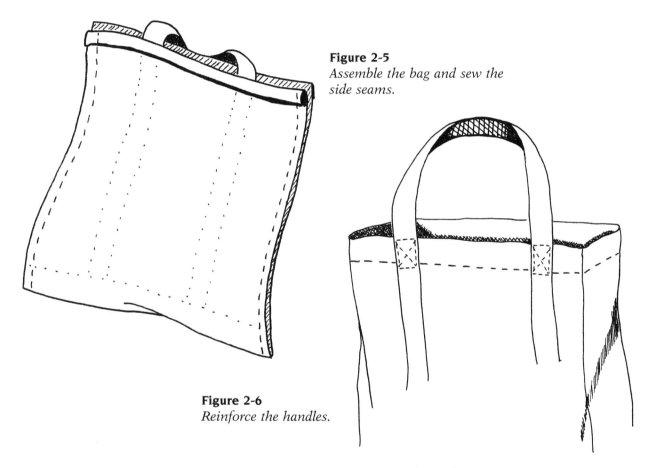

Figure 2-5
Assemble the bag and sew the side seams.

Figure 2-6
Reinforce the handles.

Fold the top edge of the bag down again 1″ (2.5cm) and stitch.

With the bag right side out, reinforce the handles at the top edge of the bag by straight stitching a square at each handle (Fig. 2-6). Edgestitch the portion of the handles that extends beyond the top edge of the bag.

To give the bag a flat bottom, follow these easy steps. First, turn the bag wrong side out. At each bottom corner, form a point by lining up the center bottom (folded edge) with the side seam (Fig. 2-7). Measure 2¼″ (5.5cm) down from each point and sew straight across the triangle that is formed. Trim these seams close to the stitching.

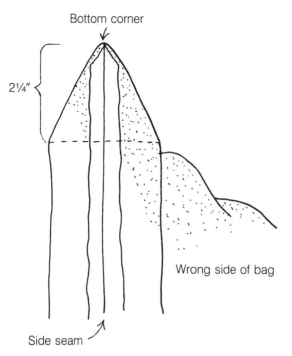

Bottom corner

2¼″

Wrong side of bag

Side seam

Figure 2-7
Give the bag a flat bottom by lining up the bottom fold with the side seam and stitching across the resulting triangle.

▶ The Not-So-Brown Bag (Fig. 2-8)

Brown-bagging encourages us to use up leftovers and thus throw away less food. Taking your food in reusable containers (salvage the plastic containers from your grocery and deli purchases instead of buying new ones) is far better than buying your lunch and having to throw away the

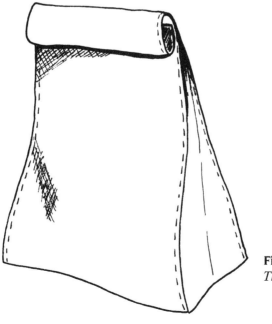

Figure 2-8
The Not-So-Brown Bag

disposable dishes, containers, and silverware used at most fast-food restaurants and cafeterias. If you want to use sandwich wrap instead of plastic containers, remember that cellulose bags and waxed paper are biodegradable and aluminum foil, of course, is recyclable, but plastic wrap is neither.

Why not add a little fun to taking your lunch by making your own washable, reusable lunch sack? Remember those lunch boxes from when you were a kid? Here's a soft, lightweight version that you can make for every family member. A bit of leftover corduroy or double-faced quilted fabric is perfect for this easy bag.

MATERIALS NEEDED

12″ × 28″ (30.5cm × 71cm) rectangle of firmly woven medium-weight
    prewashed fabric
2″ (5cm) of ⅝″-wide (1.5cm) closure tape

DIRECTIONS

Finish both 12″ (30.5cm) edges of the fabric rectangle by serging or zigzagging them or by turning the edges under ¼″ (6mm) and straight stitching.

Fold the fabric in half, right sides together, so that the short edges meet. Serge or zigzag the side seams, using a ½″ (1.3cm) seam allowance (Fig. 2-9).

At the inside bottom corners, form triangles by folding the bottom edge to the side seams (see Fig. 2-7). Measure 2¼″ (5.5cm) down from

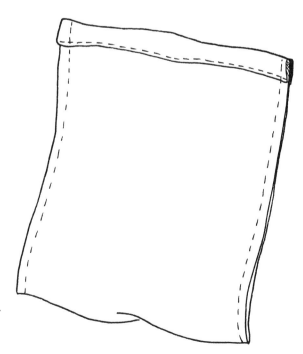

Figure 2-9
Serge or zigzag the side seams.

the point of the triangles and serge or sew straight across. Trim the seams close to the stitching.

Fold the finished top edge down ¼″ (6mm) and topstitch.

Press the creases along the sides of the bag from the bottom corners to the top edge (Fig. 2-10). Edgestitch all four creases.

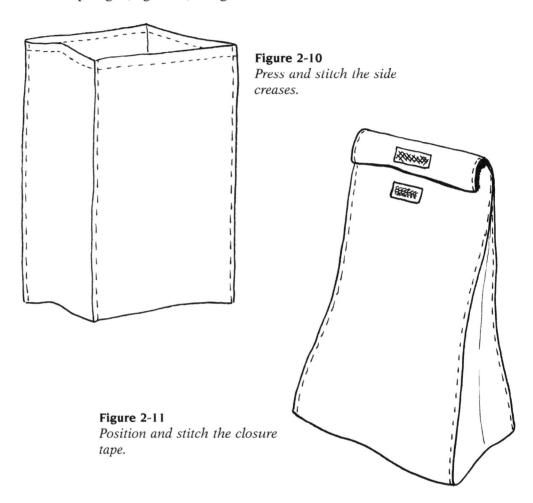

Figure 2-10
Press and stitch the side creases.

Figure 2-11
Position and stitch the closure tape.

Center 2″ (5cm) of the hook side of the closure tape at the top edge of bag (Fig. 2-11). Stitch in place. On the *opposite* side of the bag, stitch the loop side of the closure tape 2½″ (6.5cm) down from the top edge, centered from side to side.

To close the bag, fold down the top to secure the closure tape.

Fill the bag with your favorite lunch and enjoy!

▶ Mug Pack (Fig. 2-12)

Cut down on the number of Styrofoam and paper cups you use by taking your own mug to work for coffee breaks and tea time. Slip your cup into

Figure 2-12
The Mug Pack

this padded tote to protect it as you carry it. Handy pockets hold a spoon, sugar packs, and tea and coffee bags (see the Color Section).

MATERIALS NEEDED
4 pieces of firmly woven medium-weight prewashed fabric: 9″ × 19″ (23cm × 48.5cm) for the body, 7″ × 19″ (18cm × 48.5cm) for the pocket, and 2 pieces 8″ × 8″ (20.5cm × 20.5cm) for the base
2 pieces of low-loft fleece: 3½″ × 19″ (9cm × 48.5cm) and 8″ × 8″ (20.5cm × 20.5cm)
12″ (30.5cm) of decorative cord for the drawstring

DIRECTIONS
Fold the pocket piece in half lengthwise, wrong sides together, and place the strip of fleece inside. Quilt by straight stitching across the pocket in rows ¼″ (6mm) apart. Position the pocket on top of the body fabric with the lower raw edges even. Baste across the side edges of the pocket.

Create the spoon pocket by stitching two straight lines up from the bottom edge of the quilted pocket, one 3″ (7.5cm) and one 4¼″ (11cm) from the side. This results in a spoon pocket that is 1¼″ (3cm) wide (Fig. 2-13).

Fold the bag right sides together and stitch the side seam, beginning 1″ (2.5cm) from top edge and using a ½″ (1.3cm) seam allowance. Press the seam open.

Finish the seam edges by serging or zigzagging if desired.

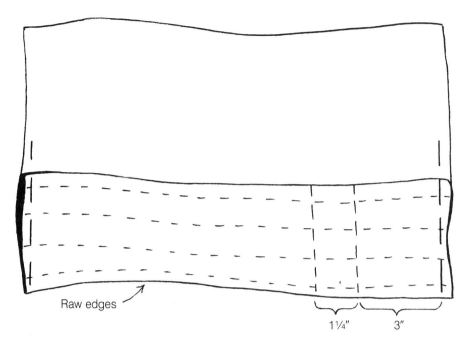

Raw edges

1¼″   3″

Figure 2-13
After basting the sides of the quilted pocket, stitch the vertical seams for the pocket divisions.

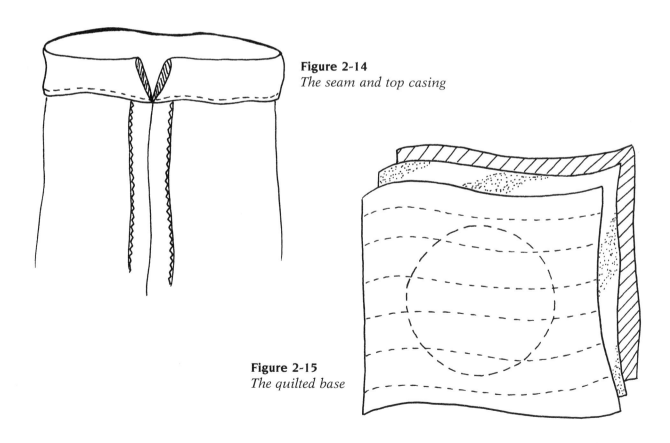

Figure 2-14
The seam and top casing

Figure 2-15
The quilted base

With the bag inside out, fold down the top edge ¼″ (6mm) and press. Fold down another ½″ (1.3cm) and stitch, leaving an opening at the seam for the cord (Fig. 2-14).

Sandwich the remaining fleece between the fabric pieces, wrong sides together. Quilt in the same manner as the pocket. From this quilted base, cut out a circle that is 6″ (15cm) in diameter (Fig. 2-15).

With right sides together and using a ¼″ (6mm) seam allowance, stitch base to the body of tote, creating the bag's bottom.

Insert the decorative cord through the casing and pull it up to close the tote.

▶ Handi-Tote (Fig. 2-16)

Figure 2-16
The Handi-Tote

Don't get caught shopping without a bag. Here's a lightweight, washable bag that folds up so that you can always have it with you (see the Color Section). Tuck it away in a purse or pocket and use it to carry home those impulse buys.

MATERIALS NEEDED
1¼ yards (1.15m) strong, lightweight durable fabric such as Supplex or ripstop nylon
Cable cord for the handle

DIRECTIONS

Cut the following pieces from the fabric:
- Two 24″ × 36″ (61cm × 91.5cm) rectangles for the body of the bag.
- One 8″ × 12″ (20.5cm × 30.5cm) for the pocket.
  Optional: Stitch together fabric strips of various colors to make a piece of fabric for the pocket.
- One 3″ × 28″ (7.5cm × 71cm) strip for the strap.

Mark a 1″ (2.5cm) buttonhole in the center of one 36″ (91.5cm) side of the body piece, 1½″ (4cm) down from the top edge. Reinforce the area on the wrong side with a small piece of fusible interfacing. Stitch the buttonhole parallel to edge.

To make the strap, fold the strip right sides together and stitch, using a ¼″ (6mm) seam allowance. Turn the piece right side out and press it, positioning the seam at the center of the back side.

Fold the pocket piece across the 8″ (20.5cm) side with right sides together and stitch the sides, leaving only a ¼″ (6mm) seam allowance (Fig. 2-17). Trim the corners and turn the pocket right side out through the bottom edge.

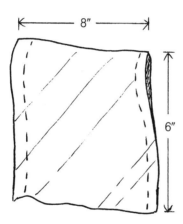

Figure 2-17
Stitch the pocket.

Position the pocket at the center lower edge of the bag with the raw edges even (Fig. 2-18). Stitch the pocket to the bag by edgestitching down the sides of the pocket.

On one of the sides, position the strap 2½″ (6.5cm) from the top edge of the bag and 1″ (2.5cm) from the lower edge, with the raw edges even (see Fig. 2-18). Fold the tote with right sides together and stitch down the side, making sure to securely catch the ends of the straps. Reinforce the straps by stitching a second time across the ends of the straps.

Stitch the lower edge of the bag, lining up the side seam across from the center of the pocket (Fig. 2-19). Catch the lower edge of the pocket as you sew.

To form the casing, turn the top edge under ¼″ (6mm). Then fold it under another ½″ (1.3cm) and stitch.

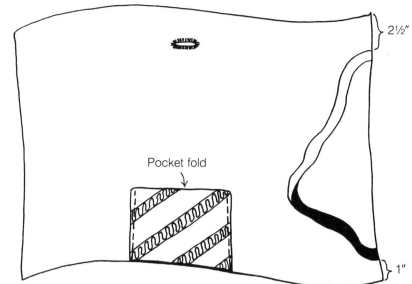

Figure 2-18
Position the pocket and straps.

Thread the cord through the casing by going through the buttonhole. Pull the cord to close the bag.

To pack the bag, fold the sides lengthwise toward the center. Fold down from the top until the bag is the same size as the pocket. Turn the pocket inside out to contain the bag (Fig. 2-20).

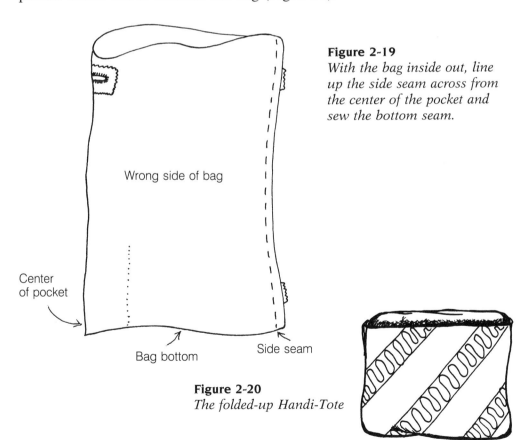

Figure 2-19
With the bag inside out, line up the side seam across from the center of the pocket and sew the bottom seam.

Figure 2-20
The folded-up Handi-Tote

Chapter 3
From One to Another

*Turning Adult Garments
into Children's Clothes
and Infant Items*

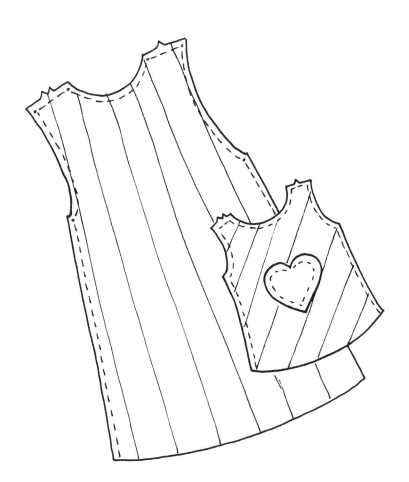

ONE DEFINITION of recycling is using one item to make another. There is no better way to do this than making baby or children items from adult garments. A discarded adult garment usually has more than ample fabric to create a brand-new outfit for a baby or child.

A newborn's layette should include several buntings and nightgowns so that there's always one to wear, even with several in the laundry. A bunting is similar to a nightgown but is made of a warm, cuddly fabric, such as fleece or flannel, and includes a drawstring bottom so that it can be worn outdoors.

An adult T-shirt is the perfect choice of materials for a baby's nightgown, and a sweatshirt is ideal for a bunting.

▶ Infant Nightgown or Bunting (Fig. 3-1)

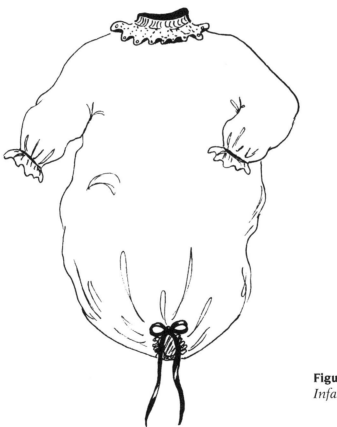

Figure 3-1
Infant Bunting

MATERIALS NEEDED

Adult T-shirt of 100% cotton that is soft and absorbent (Make sure that most of the shirt is in good condition and free of stains.)

Ribbing (If the shirt's ribbing still has stretch to it, you can reuse it. If

not, purchase new ribbing or use some left over from another
  project.)
Lace or trim equal to diameter of the neck edge
¾ yard (68.5cm) of ¼" (6mm) clear elastic
22" (56cm) of ribbon or cord for the drawstring on the bunting

DIRECTIONS

If you are reusing the shirt's neck ribbing, carefully remove it from
the T-shirt and trim it to 3" (7.5cm) wide. Press, *without* using steam, to
straighten the ribbing.

Spread out the T-shirt so that it lies flat. You may need to cut the
shirt open at the side seams. Cut out the front and back of the nightgown
according to the pattern (Fig. 3-2). Avoid any areas that are worn or
stained.

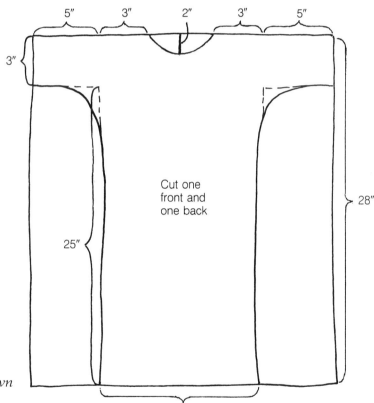

Figure 3-2
Pattern for the Infant Nightgown

Place the front and back right sides together and stitch the shoulder
seams.

Baste the lace or trim around the neck edge with the raw edges even.
Cut the length of the ribbing to equal two-thirds of the neck opening.
Stitch the ribbing into a circle and make sure it is large enough to go

over the baby's head. Fold the ribbing strip in half with the stretch going around the neck.

Divide the ribbing in quarters and mark each section with a pin. Place the right side of the folded ribbing next to the right side of the neck edge with the raw edges even.

Stitch with a serger or use a stretch stitch on the machine. Gently stretch the ribbing to match the marks to center front and back and to the shoulder seams.

Turn under the sleeve edge ¼″ (6mm) twice and topstitch it to create a hem.

Position 3″ (7.5cm) of clear elastic on the wrong side of the nightgown, 1″ (2.5cm) from the hemmed sleeve edge, and zigzag it in place, stretching it across the width of the sleeve.

Stitch the underarm seams and side seams with a serger or stretch stitch, making sure hemmed edges of sleeve are even.

To add a drawstring and create a bunting, mark a ¾″ (2cm) horizontal buttonhole in the center front, 2¼″ (5.5cm) from the lower edge. Reinforce the wrong side of the buttonhole area with fusible interfacing. Stitch the buttonhole.

Fold the lower edge to the wrong side, first ¼″ (6mm) and then 1½″ (4cm). Stitch the hem in place 1¼″ (3cm) from the edge to form the casing.

Insert the ribbon or cord through the casing, then pull it up and tie it in a bow. Buntings and nightgowns should be long enough and loose enough to give the baby ample room for movement.

▶ Kids' Clothes

DIRECTIONS

Baby clothes are not the only items you can make from adult clothing. Look through your closet and pull out the garments you no longer wear. You will find that you have yards of fabric to use for the older children in the house.

Take a close look at the clothing you've selected to make over. Check for moth holes, stains, or tears and make sure that the bulk of the fabric is in good condition. Look at the garment critically to make sure it is usable. If you don't like the look of the fabric, try using it with the wrong side out. If the inside is more pleasing, there's no rule that says you can't use it.

When selecting a pattern for this project, choose simple designs that use only a few pieces. In general, the new pattern should not contain any pieces larger than the pieces of the original garment. New garments that require large amounts of fabrics (such as full skirts or long dresses) will probably not work as a remade garment.

Preparing the fabric is a simple matter of taking apart the garment after it has been washed or dry-cleaned. Begin by ripping open the seams of the garment. Do this carefully since the fabric may not be as strong as when it was new. After taking the garment apart, press each piece. You may want to mark the right and wrong sides to be sure you are consistent when cutting out the new pattern. Using chalk or a basting thread, mark the straight grain line of the piece so that you can cut the fabric correctly and ensure that the new garment will hang properly.

When laying out the new pattern pieces, try to use the corresponding pieces of the garment; for example, cut the sleeve pattern from the sleeves and the front from the front. Doing this will make planning your layout easier, and the pieces will usually fit. If you find that you need to do some piecing to have enough fabric to cut the new pattern, try to do so in an inconspicuous place. Under the arm, at the back waist where a belt might cover it, or at the side of the garment are good locations for piecing. Be sure to match the grain lines of the pieces you are putting together so that they will blend as much as possible.

The diagrams in Figures 3-3, 3-4, and 3-5 give some ideas of pattern layouts for restyling one garment into another. This is just the beginning of what you could do with fabric you already have hanging in your closet. Just use your imagination and let the sky be the limit and you can make a brand-new child's wardrobe for practically nothing.

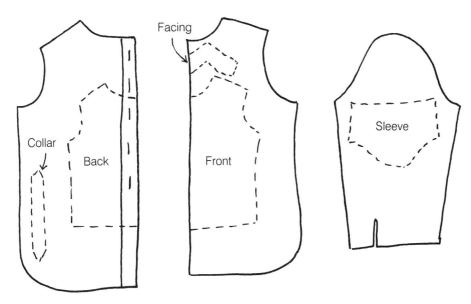

Figure 3-3
Make a child's blouse from an adult's shirt.

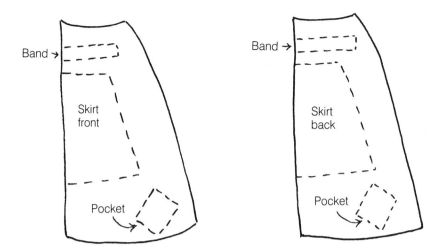

Figure 3-4
Use a woman's skirt to make one for a child.

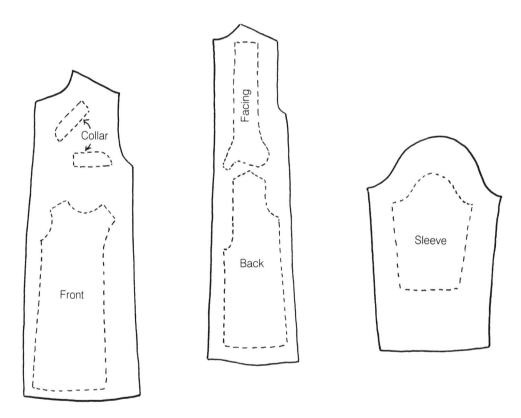

Figure 3-5
Cut a child's coat from an adult's overcoat.

▶ Cloth Diapers (Fig. 3-6)

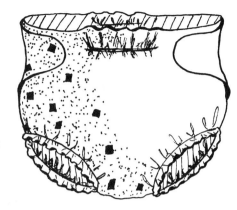

Figure 3-6
Cloth diapers help the environment.

Everyone has heard about the controversy involving disposable diapers versus cloth diapers. After they are thrown away, disposable diapers do not decompose, and they add tons of refuse to our landfills every year. Even the new disposables that claim to be biodegradable will only partially decompose over the years. Disposables are certainly more convenient and easier to deal with after changing baby, but we need to consider if this convenience is worth the high price that future generations will have to pay.

Using cloth diapers for only part of the time will help to reduce the trash problem that disposables cause. A cloth diaper doesn't have to be just a large square of cloth folded and pinned around the baby. Make a cute fitted diaper that won't droop or sag with Velcro-type closures and help preserve the environment while still having some of the conveniences of disposables. This diaper is also a wonderful gift for new parents.

MATERIALS NEEDED (makes two diapers)
½ yard (45.5cm) of 45″ (114.5cm) printed flannel
1 yard (91.5cm) of 27″ (68.5cm) 100% cotton diaper flannel
¼″ (6mm) clear elastic
5″ (12.5cm) closure tape

DIRECTIONS
Using the measurements given in Figure 3-7, cut one fitted diaper shape from the printed flannel. Be sure to transfer markings A, B, C and D to both layers of fabric.

From the diaper flannel cut one fitted diaper shape (see Fig. 3-7), transferring all the markings, and two or three 5″ × 11″ (12.5cm × 28cm) center panels.

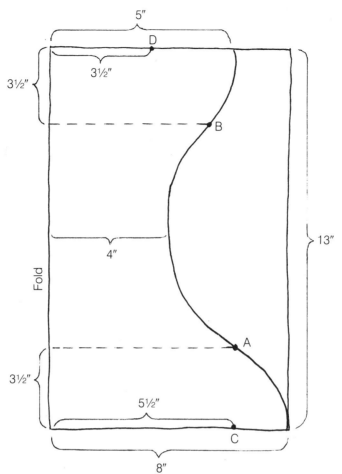

5"

D

3½"

3½"

B

Fold

4"

13"

A

3½"

5½"

C

8"

Figure 3-7
Pattern for the diaper

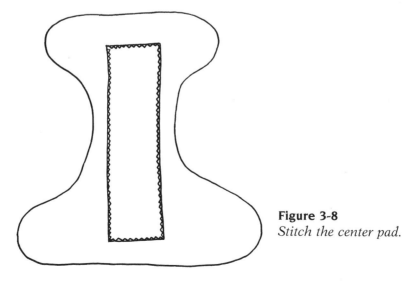

Figure 3-8
Stitch the center pad.

Stack center panels together and pin them at each edge. If you want to increase the absorbency of the panel, add extra layers. Put two or three extra layers on the front half of the panel for boys, or center two or three extra layers in the middle of the panel for girls.

Position the panels in the center of the wrong side of the shaped diaper flannel piece (Fig. 3-8). Stitch around all the edges of the panel using a narrow zigzag stitch, securing the edges to the diaper flannel.

Place the diaper flannel piece and printed flannel piece right sides together and stitch with a ¼″ (6mm) seam, leaving a 3″ (7.5cm) opening at the back upper edge. Turn the diaper through the opening and press it. Edgestitch all around and stitch the opening closed.

Stitch the soft side of the closure tape on the side extensions on the front of the diaper. Place 2″ (5cm) pieces of the rough side of the tape on the wrong side of the tabs at the back of the diaper (Fig. 3-9). When washing the diapers, fold the rough side of the closure tab over on the diaper to keep it from sticking to other items in the washing machine.

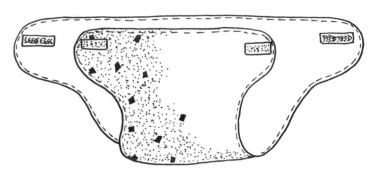

Figure 3-9
Place the closure tape strips that will secure the diaper.

Cut the ¼″ (6mm) clear elastic (which is soft to the touch and won't irritate the baby's skin) in the following sizes: 4″ (10cm) for the front, 7″ (18cm) for the back, and 6″ (15cm) for the legs. Stitch through the middle of the elastic with a medium zigzag stitch while stretching it to fit between the indicated marks (A to B = legs; C = back; D = front).

▶ Baby Burp Cloth (Fig. 3-10)

DIRECTIONS
The reality of taking care of babies includes needing a little protection for your clothing as you hold the little darlings. A burp cloth to throw over your shoulder when feeding or holding the baby is easy to make from a worn-out towel or sheet. In addition to the towel or sheet, you'll need a rectangle of fabric 11½″ × 32″ (29.5cm × 81.5cm). Check your discarded linens for any usable fabric.

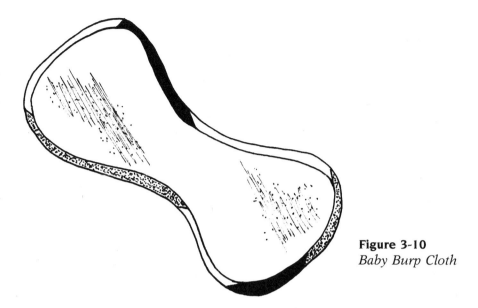

Figure 3-10
Baby Burp Cloth

Cut the towel or sheet the same size as the fabric. On each piece, round the corners and shape the center portion of the rectangle so that it curves in (Fig. 3-11). This part will fit over your shoulder.

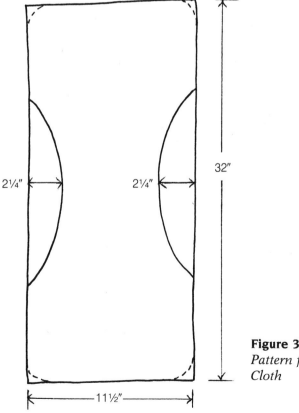

2¼″   2¼″

32″

Figure 3-11
Pattern for the Baby Burp Cloth

11½″

Place the toweling and the fabric portion *wrong sides together* and baste about ⅛″ (3mm) from the edges. Using packaged double-folded bias tape, bind the edges of the cloth. This is a great time to use up the odds and ends of packaged tape that you have left over from previous projects. Stitch the pieces together to form a single piece of tape long enough to go all the way around the cloth. When joining the pieces of tape, sew them at an angle to make the seam less conspicuous and easier to stitch over (Fig. 3-12). To do this, place the two pieces of tape, right sides together, at right angles and stitch at a 45-degree angle. The second piece of tape folds up and across the first one, forming a straight line of tape.

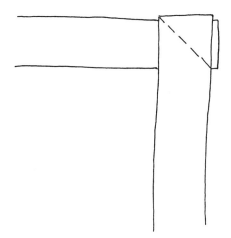

Figure 3-12
Join the strips of bias tape.

Chapter 4
Scrap-Happy

*Using Scraps to Make Quilts
and Small Projects*

AN INEVITABLE by-product of sewing is all the leftover fabric you will accumulate. It's almost impossible to use every bit of fabric bought for a project, but even if you have only small swatches remaining, there are ways to use them. Our grandmothers kept a ragbag or a scrap basket and always had small pieces for a new project.

Quilts may be the first thing that comes to mind when we think of scraps of fabric—those beautifully stitched patterns made from hundreds of tiny swatches. Today, we purchase new fabric and cut it into small pieces so that we can sew it together again to make a big piece! It's not only fun and creative, but we can plan the colors and patterns so that we actually make a work of art, as well as a practical project.

In years past, quilts were made out of scraps and remnants from the ragbag. Returning to that method can be very gratifying. Not only will you have the satisfaction of using all of your fabric, but the results will be a pleasing combination of charm, beauty, and personality. In addition, you can piece a quilt without using a great deal of two precious commodities—time and money.

▶ Practical Piecing

DIRECTIONS

When you have finished a current sewing project, cut the remaining scraps into squares. The size of the square is not important, but there are a few things to consider. Be consistent in the size you cut until you are finished with a particular pieced project. The larger the square, the faster the project will be pieced, but the squares shouldn't be too large because you'll want to incorporate fabric from projects with very small leftovers. A 4″–6″ (10cm–15cm) square is a good choice. If you have a square ruler, cutting the fabric the size of the ruler will make the cutting go faster, especially if you use a rotary cutter.

Place a basket or box near the sewing machine and throw the squares into it. Keep fabrics of similar fiber content together, pinning them with a safety pin until you are ready to use them. When you have a few spare moments, stitch several blocks together. Before you know it, you will have finished a project that cost you almost nothing.

In traditional hand-piecing, seam allowances are ¼″ (6mm) and are pressed to the side to avoid putting stress on the seam and to increase the durability of the piece. When machine-piecing, the seam allowance should also be ¼″ (6mm), but you may press the seam to the side or press it open to reduce the bulk.

When piecing the squares together, don't worry about the print or color combinations. Concentrate only on contrast (Fig. 4-1). Try to intermingle the lights and darks together to keep the contrast distinctive. When you have completed the project, look at it with a critical eye. If you

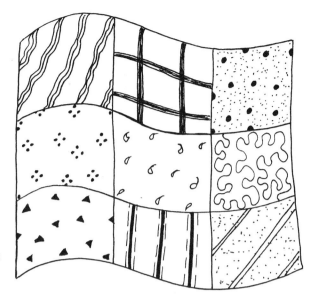

Figure 4-1
Square-to-square quilt pattern

are not completely happy with the color combinations, use a tan fabric dye (available in grocery stores and craft stores) and overdye the entire piece to give it a soft, muted look. You'll be amazed at how well the colors will blend and how wonderful they will look together.

▶ Pieced Lap Throw

DIRECTIONS

When you make patchwork squares, you can vary the design instead of making the traditional squares stitched to squares. With only a little more effort, you can plan a distinctive piece with a lot of personality. For example, the lap throw shown in the Color Section looks much more intricately pieced than it is. It's machine-quilted using a technique I call *layered quilting*: squares stitched together with smaller squares layered on top (Fig. 4-2). The smaller squares are turned on their points and appliquéd in place with a decorative stitch.

You can make this quilt any size you want by adding more squares. The chart below shows the size of quilts needed for different bed sizes, so you can determine for yourself how many squares you will need.

SIZES FOR PIECED LAP THROW

Type	Size Needed for Bedspread	Size Needed for Comforter
Twin	81″ × 110″ (205.5cm × 279.5cm)	69″ × 90″ (175.5cm × 228.5cm)
Full	96″ × 110″ (244cm × 279.5cm)	84″ × 90″ (213.5cm × 228.5cm)
Queen	102″ × 120″ (259cm × 305cm)	90″ × 95″ (228.5cm × 241.5cm)
King	120″ × 120″ (305cm × 305cm)	95″ × 106″ (241.5cm × 269cm)

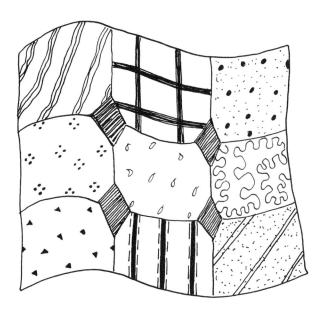

Figure 4-2
Layered squares

After stitching the desired number of squares together, you are ready to place the smaller squares on the pieced top. Cut the smaller squares half the size of the larger squares. The lap throw shown in the Color Section has 6″ (15cm) squares for the background and 3″ (7.5cm) squares appliquéd on top.

Back the smaller squares with fusible web and fuse them to the quilt. Turn the squares on point and fuse one square over each intersection where four of the large squares come together. Don't forget to fuse half-squares (triangles) around the edges. A decorative stitch will be used around the raw edges of the small squares when quilting. If you want the smaller squares to have a finished edge, add a ¼″ (6mm) seam allowance to them before cutting them out. Fold under the seam allowance before fusing the square in place.

Next, cut strips for the borders. You may make them in any width and add as many as you like to frame the pieced area. The quilt in Figure 4-3 has borders that were cut 3½″ (9cm) wide.

Layer the pieced top with quilt batting or filler and a backing fabric. Use purchased quilt batting as a filler or look around the house to see if you have something else that might be appropriate, such as a blanket.

Most blankets begin to show wear around the edges first, leaving the rest of the area still useful. Using a blanket is similar to using quilt batting, and you'll want to treat it in the same way. Make sure that the blanket is washable if you plan to wash the finished quilt. Trim the blanket to the size you want, squaring up the corners. If you have several smaller pieces of fleece left over from other projects, stitch them together to make a larger piece. The pieces should be of similar weight and loft. Place the pieces edge to edge and stitch them together with a medium zigzag stitch

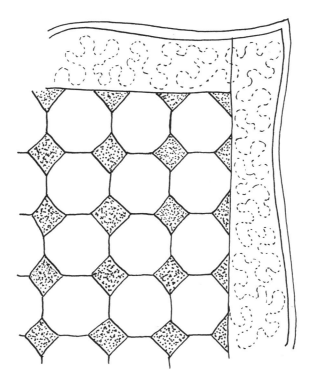

Figure 4-3
A bordered quilt

or a running stitch (Fig. 4-4). Sew enough pieces together to make the size filler piece that you need.

Using safety pins to baste the layers together, start in the center and work out to the edges, keeping all the layers smooth and wrinkle-free.

With a walking foot or an even-feed foot, begin quilting in the center area of the quilt. Stitch around the edges of the small squares with a decorative stitch (Fig. 4-5). A feather stitch or blanket stitch is a good choice for this, but any favorite stitch will work.

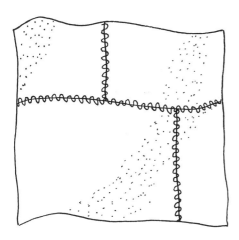

Figure 4-4
Pieced fleece for the filler

Figure 4-5
Quilting with decorative stitches

After stitching around the smaller squares, if desired, you can use a straight stitch to stitch in the ditch on the seam lines that join the large squares together.

Stitch in the ditch along the border seam at the edge of the pieced area. You can use any quilting design you wish in the border section. The quilt in Figure 4-5 has free-motion stitching across the borders. The walking foot was replaced with a darning foot, the feed dogs were dropped, and the quilt was moved freely to produce a random pattern of stitching.

When you have completed all the quilting, bind the edges with an easy double binding. Sometimes called a French binding, double binding provides a stable outer edge to any quilt. Cut a bias strip of fabric 3½″ (9cm) wide and long enough to go around the quilt. If necessary, piece the strip until you have the required length.

Fold the binding strip in half lengthwise, wrong sides together, and press. Place the strip at the edge of the quilt with the raw edges even. Stitch, using a ½″ (1.3cm) seam allowance. Fold to the back and stitch, using a blind stitch or a decorative stitch (Fig. 4-6).

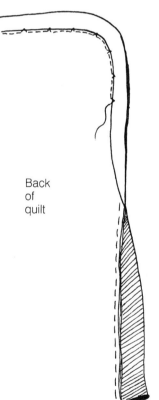

Back
of
quilt

Figure 4-6
French binding

▶ Surprise Log Cabin

DIRECTIONS

The log cabin pattern is an enduring favorite that has been popular since pioneer days. It lends itself easily to scrap piecing and has so many variations that you can change the design of the quilt just by rearranging the blocks.

Instead of cutting your remnants into the usual squares, cut them into strips to begin building your log cabin. In traditional log-cabin quilts, the center block is usually made from red fabric to symbolize the hearth of the home. So, select a red remnant for the center squares. Cut the strips that make up the logs forming the cabin around the hearth from light and dark fabrics. When you make a surprise log cabin, there is very little planning done beforehand. Simply cut your fabrics into strips and divide them into a light pile and a dark pile. As you build the block, pull a strip from the appropriate stack and stitch it on. To make the pattern a real surprise, put the strips into paper bags and pull them out potluck. The surprise is how well the fabrics work together in this future family heirloom.

To make a 7″ (18cm) finished block, cut the strips 1½″ (4cm) wide. Cut them as long as your fabric scraps allow. If necessary, piece them together as you go.

Building the block is as easy as straight stitching. *Note:* all stitching is done right sides together with a ¼″ (6mm) seam allowance.

Begin with the hearth. Cut a square (A) from the red strip. Place a light strip (B) face down on the square and stitch the squares together (Fig. 4-7). With scissors or a rotary cutter, trim away the excess fabric, making the light strip the same size as the red square. Do this carefully; it must be a straight edge.

Next, place a light strip (C) across the edge formed by the first two pieces (Fig. 4-8). Stitch and trim it even with squares A and B.

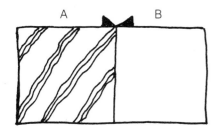

Figure 4-7
Log cabin, step #1

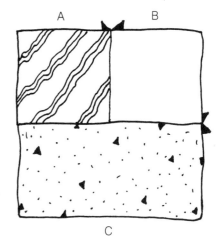

Figure 4-8
Log cabin, step #2

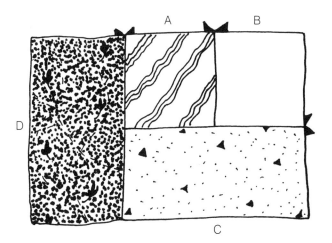

Figure 4-9
Log cabin, step #3

The next strip you use will be a dark one placed on the edge formed by squares A and C (Fig. 4-9).

Continue this stitching in a clockwise manner, alternating two strips of light and two strips of dark until the block is completed (six light and six dark strips) (Fig. 4-10). Don't forget to trim each strip carefully to size after stitching.

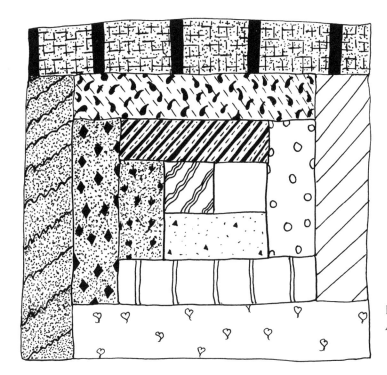

Figure 4-10
A completed log cabin block

If you come to a point where your strip is not long enough for the edge it is to be stitched to, simply take another strip (light to light or dark to dark) and seam them together to get more length. In the overall scheme of things, these pieced portions will only add character rather than detract from the beauty of the design.

The completed blocks are usually set together without sashing or borders to form a number of different patterns. Figure 4-11 shows two of the more popular ways to set the blocks together to form different patterns. Use your imagination and see what else you can come up with.

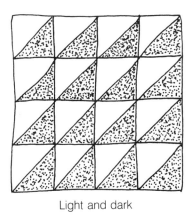 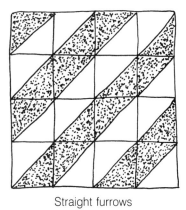

Light and dark   Straight furrows

Figure 4-11
Variations for setting the quilt blocks

▶ Country Table Runner

DIRECTIONS
Shown in the Color Section (and in Fig. 4-12), this table runner is made with four log cabin blocks stitched side by side and set in the furrow design. A 2½″ (6.5cm) border strip is added to each side of the row of blocks. To complete the shape of the runner, add a triangle at each end.

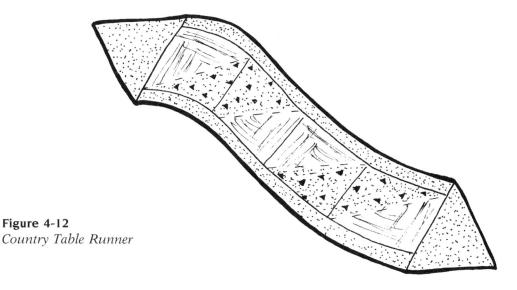

Figure 4-12
Country Table Runner

After piecing the blocks and stitching them together with the borders and end pieces, cut the backing the same size as the complete piece. To stitch piping around the edges, place covered cord along the edge of the pieced top with the raw edges even. Place the backing right side down on top of the runner. Using a ¼″ (6mm) seam allowance, stitch around all the edges close to the piping. Leave an opening for turning.

Trim the seams, turn, and press. Topstitch along the inside of the piping, closing the opening as you stitch.

▶ Cinnamon-Scented Coaster

Cut ¾″-wide (2cm) strips to make miniature blocks, allowing you to use even smaller scraps. The results are beautiful tiny versions of the traditional block, perfect for small projects, such as the Cinnamon-scented Coasters pictured in the Color Section.

MATERIALS NEEDED
4 miniature log cabin blocks placed as shown (Fig. 4-13)

Figure 4-13
Cinnamon-Scented Coaster

Figure 4-14
Sprinkle the cinnamon inside the coaster before edgestitching.

Make every last scrap count! Use leftover fabrics to create this colorful layer-quilted Pieced Lap Throw (Chapter 4).

Transform little bits of fabric into pretty hair ornaments in just a few minutes. Then, using leftover ribbon, make a hanging organizer to keep your "pretties" in order (Chapter 4). The Strip Belt at right is another way to use up small pieces of fabric (Chapter 4).

Coordinate your travel needs by using recycled fabrics to make a curling iron carrier, a cosmetics bag, and this handy pocket purse that holds tissue and change (Chapter 4).

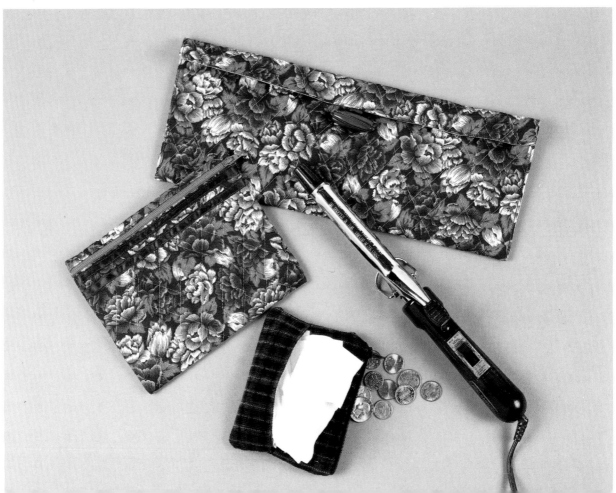

Find yards of colorful fabric by salvaging old neckties and using them to make yardage for vests, jackets, pillows, and more. Instructions for this Tie It Up! vest are in Chapter 6.

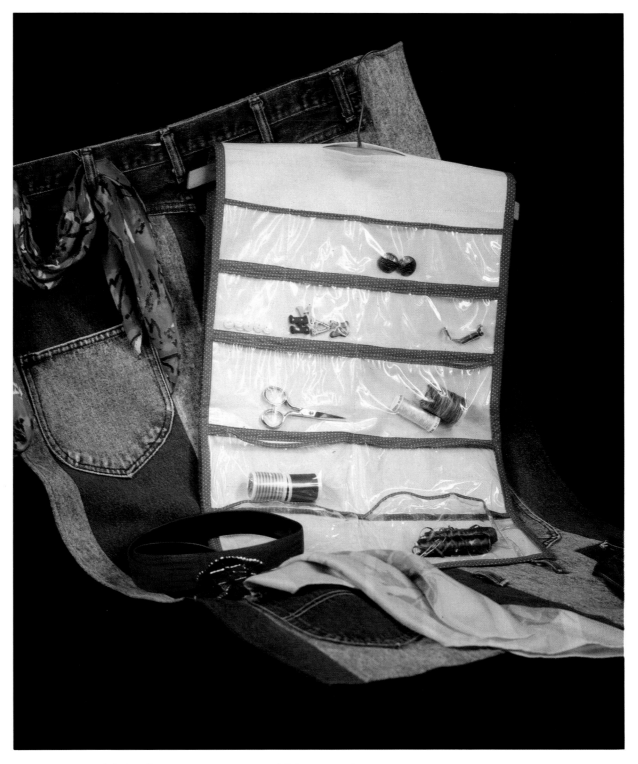

Organize your life (and use up extra pieces of fabirc, vinyl, and denim) by creating these hanging-pocket organizers that can hold everything from sewing supplies to kitchen gadgets. (You'll find instructions for the denim Back-Pocket Organizer in Chapter 6 and those for the vinyl Hanging See-Through Organizer in Chapter 10.)

Design a one-of-a-kind garment like this Remnant Jacket (Chapter 5) by using remnants of fine fabric and pulling the look together with machine embellishment and decorations.

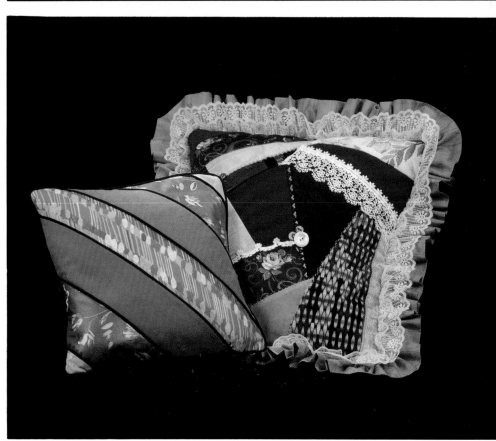

Brighten your home and recycle at the same time. These piped and pieced pillows were created from odds and ends of decorator fabrics (instructions are in Chapter 7). Other home sewing ideas include giving an old quilt new life by sewing a duvet cover using sheets or extra fabric (Chapter 7).

Take a bag with you wherever you go. This drawstring Handi-Tote (shown unfolded at left) folds up into a pocket so you'll be ready for those impulse buys (Chapter 2).

Save trees by avoiding the store's paper or plastic bags and shopping with your own Sturdy Canvas Shopping Bag (Chapter 2). The bag's reinforced base will help you carry even the heaviest loads.

*Use up those extra buttons pil-
ing up in your sewing room to
refurbish a vest or create these
unique gold-painted Button
Cluster Pins (Chapter 8). A favorite decorative button can be
used as the closure for this belt
that is embellished with machine stitching (Chapter 4).*

Use small scraps of fabric to create cozy items for your home, such as this Country Table Runner and Cinnamon-Scented Coaster (Chapter 4). The padded Mug Pack (Chapter 2) provides a tote for your reusable coffee mug, eliminating the need for Styrofoam or plastic cups.

Show off your favorite stitching techniques on this Signature Vest (Chapter 5). The patchwork look is achieved by embellishing small swatches of fabric.

Square of backing fabric the same size as the combined pieced blocks
Thin fleece the same size as the backing
1–2 teaspoons of ground cinnamon

DIRECTIONS

Place the backing right side down on the pieced square with a square of fleece on the wrong side of the backing fabric.

Stitch around all sides, leaving an opening for turning.

Trim the corners and seam allowances and turn to the right side. Sprinkle the ground cinnamon into the coaster over the fleece (Fig. 4-14). When a mug filled with a hot liquid is placed on the coaster, the warm cinnamon will release a pleasant aroma.

Edgestitch all the edges, closing the opening as you sew.

Stitch in the ditch on the seams connecting the blocks. The stitching will form a cross.

Leftover pieces of fabric are perfect for small projects that are practical and make great gifts, too. The following are a few ideas for projects that are quick to make and take only a few bits of fabric.

▶ Tissue/Change Purse (Fig. 4-15)

MATERIALS NEEDED
4 small pieces of fabric
7″ (18cm) zipper

Figure 4-15
Tissue/Change Purse

DIRECTIONS

Cut the fabric pieces as shown in Figure 4-16.

Fold pieces C and D in half across the 5¾" (14.5cm) side and edgestitch each of them next to the fold. Place them on top of piece B with the folded edges meeting at the placement line. Baste around all the edges ⅛" (3mm) from the raw edge.

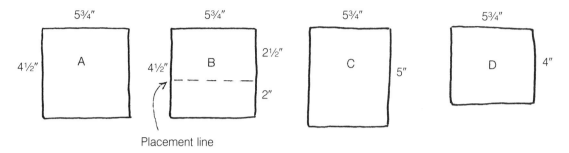

Figure 4-16
Pattern pieces for the purse

Place the zipper face down on the right side of the 5¾" (14.5cm) edge of piece A. Stitch next to the coil with a ½" (1.3cm) seam allowance, using a zipper foot. Place layered piece B on the other side of the zipper, right sides together (Fig. 4-17). Stitch with a ½" (1.3cm) seam allowance next to the coil, using a zipper foot. If desired, turn over and topstitch the fabric on the right side next to the zipper teeth.

Place pieces A and B right sides together with the *zipper halfway open*. Stitch down the sides and across the bottom, using a narrow zigzag stitch

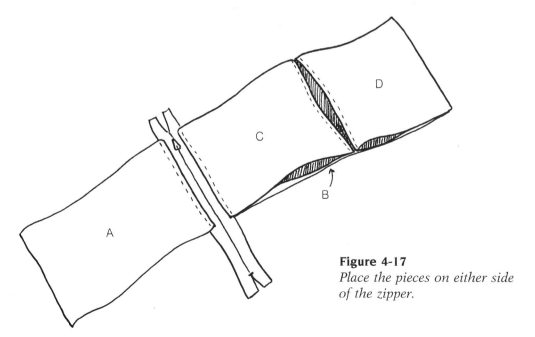

Figure 4-17
Place the pieces on either side of the zipper.

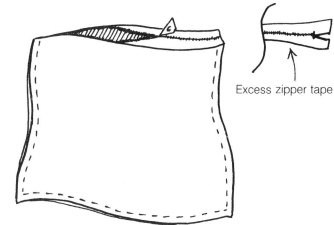

Excess zipper tape

Figure 4-18
*Stitch the sides and bottom
with the zipper partially open.*

and a ¼" (6mm) seam allowance. Trim off the excess zipper tape (Fig. 4-18).

Turn through the zippered opening.

▶ Accordion Hair Bow (Fig. 4-19)

Experiment with different sizes of bows for different looks with this stylish hair ornament. Bows are so easy to make that you can have one to match every outfit (see the Color Section).

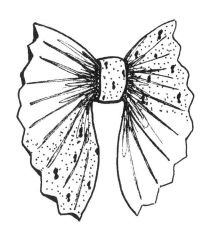

Figure 4-19
Accordion Hair Bow

MATERIALS NEEDED
Light- to medium-weight fabric
Barrette clip

DIRECTIONS
Cut two pieces of fabric according to the diagram (Fig. 4-20).
Cut one rectangle 1½" × 3" (4cm × 7.5cm).

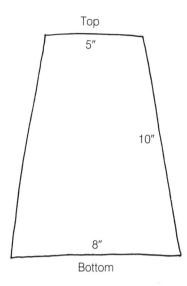

Top

5″

10″

8″

Bottom

Figure 4-20
Pattern for the Hair Bow

Place the large pieces right sides together. Stitch, using a ¼″ (6mm) seam allowance. Leave an opening at the bottom edge.

Trim the corners at an angle, turn the piece right side out, and press it. Edgestitch around all sides, closing the opening as you sew.

Press the long edges of the small rectangle under to meet at the center of the wrong side of the fabric. Fold with right sides together and stitch the short ends together to form a loop. Turn the loop right side out.

Pleat the bow from top to bottom using an accordion fold.

Put the folded bow through the loop and adjust the folds evenly.

Stitch or glue the barrette clip onto the back of the bow.

▶ Hair Ornament Holder (Fig. 4-21)

Keep your bows and headbands neat and organized with a pretty hanger that's easy to make. Made of 2″-wide (5cm) ribbon, the holder takes only two yards (1.84m) and a few minutes to put together (see the Color Section).

MATERIALS NEEDED
1½ yards (1.38m) of 2″-wide (5cm) grosgrain ribbon
8″–10″ (20.5cm–25.5cm) of narrow ribbon or cord
Assorted buttons
Hot glue gun

DIRECTIONS
Cut a piece of ribbon 13″ (33cm) long. Fold each end in to the center, overlapping one end 1½″ (4cm). Tie the ribbon together tightly at its cen-

Figure 4-21
This Hair Ornament Holder has a loop at the bottom for headbands.

ter with narrow ribbon or cord to form one bow. This bow will be sewn at the top of the holder.

Hem the top edge of remaining ribbon by turning it under ¼″ (6mm) twice and stitching.

Form a hanging loop by folding 4″ (10cm) of cord or narrow ribbon in half and stitching it to the back of the remaining ribbon strip at its top center edge.

Stitch the bow you created to the ribbon strip at its center top edge, just below the hanging loop. Using a hot glue gun, glue assorted buttons at the center of the bow.

To form the headband holder at the lower edge of the ribbon, turn under the bottom edge ¼″ (6mm) and then fold 2″–2½″ (5cm–6.5cm) of the ribbon to the wrong side. Stitch across the fold to secure the loop.

▶ Curling Iron Traveler (Fig. 4-22)

Using a small piece of leftover quilted fabric and a portion of a discarded ironing board cover, make this handy travel bag for a curling iron (see the Color Section). You can put your curling iron away warm and pack it directly into your suitcase. Check your linen cabinet to see if you have an extra placemat to use instead of the quilted outer fabric.

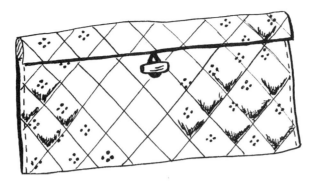

Figure 4-22
Curling Iron Traveler

MATERIALS NEEDED

Quilted fabric, 12½″ × 14″ (31.5cm × 35.5cm)

Heat-resistant fabric (ironing board cover) for the lining, 12″ × 14″ (30.5cm × 35.5cm)

¼″ (6mm) ribbon 3″ (7.5cm) long

Decorative button

DIRECTIONS

Make a loop of ribbon and place it on the right side at the center of a 14″ (35.5cm) edge of the quilted fabric, with the raw edges even (Fig. 4-23).

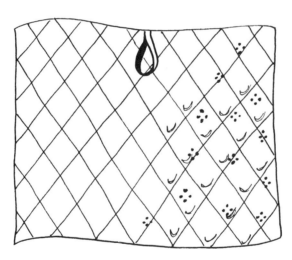

Figure 4-23
Make a loop for the hook.

Place both fabric and lining rectangles right sides together. Stitch around all the edges, leaving a 4″ (10cm) opening on one side.

Trim the corners and turn the bag through the opening. Edgestitch all the edges, closing the opening as you go.

Fold up the bottom edge (the edge without the loop) 5″ (12.5cm), forming a pocket (Fig. 4-24). Stitch over the previous edgestitching at the sides to secure the pocket.

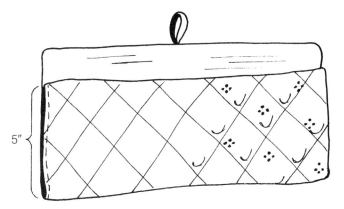

Figure 4-24
Fold up the edge to form a pocket.

5″

Sew a decorative button at the center, about 2″ (5cm) down from the edge. Fold the top down to form a flap, slipping the loop over the button to secure it.

▶ Easy Cosmetic Bag (Fig. 4-25)

This bag goes together in minutes and can be made in any size for any purpose. It makes a great companion for the Curling Iron Traveler. The directions include dimensions for the size shown in the Color Section, as well as for a slightly larger size.

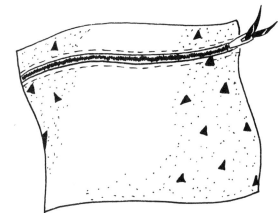

Figure 4-25
Easy Cosmetic Bag

MATERIALS NEEDED
Rectangle of medium- to heavy-weight fabric (denim, quilted fabric, chintz, etc.), 8″ × 10″ or 14″ × 16″ (20.5cm × 25.5cm or 35.5cm × 40.5cm)
Zipper, at least 2″ (5cm) longer than the shorter side of the fabric
Optional: Decorative trim or ribbon equal to two times the shorter side of the rectangle

DIRECTIONS

Stitch the zipper to the shorter sides of the rectangle by placing it face down on the right side of the fabric and stitching it next to the coils (Fig. 4-26). The zipper should extend at least 1″ (2.5cm) beyond the end of the fabric. If desired, you may topstitch next to the zipper coils on the right side of the fabric or apply a decorative trim or ribbon along the edges of the opening.

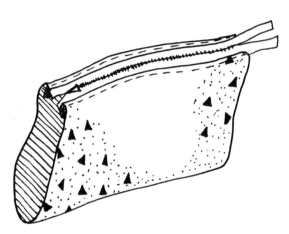

Figure 4-26
Attach the zipper.

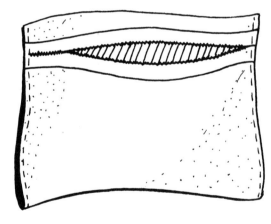

Figure 4-27
Fold the fabric so that the zipper is at the front of the bag, not at the top.

Turn the fabric wrong side out and fold it so that the zipper is near the top, but not *on* the top of the bag (Fig. 4-27). *The zipper should be open.*

Stitch the side seams, using a ¼″ (6mm) seam allowance and sewing over the zipper tape on both sides. Trim the ends of the zipper tape even with the bag.

Turn the bag through the zippered opening.

▶ **Strip Belt** (Fig. 4-28)

A 3″–5″ (9cm–12.5cm) strip of fabric is a belt just waiting to be made. However, the strip of fabric that you have available may not match or coordinate with your new outfit. This was the case with the Strip Belt pictured in the Color Section. The fabric is yellow-green and I needed a belt to wear with a navy dress. I decided to embellish the fabric with navy and fuchsia, stitching decorative cords and yarns on it and adding navy

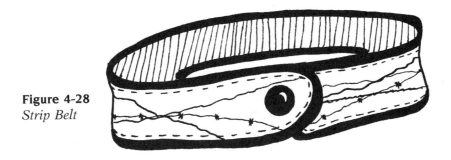

Figure 4-28
Strip Belt

piping around the edges; thus, I was not only able to wear the belt with the navy dress, but it really brightened up the outfit.

MATERIALS NEEDED

2 strips of fabric, 3″ (7.5cm) wide and the length of your waist plus 4″ (10cm)
2 strips of interfacing the same size as the fabric strips
Enough cotton cording to edge the entire belt and bias strips of fabric to cover the cording
Closure tape
One large decorative button
Decorative threads in desired colors
Decorative yarns and cords in desired colors
Nylon thread

DIRECTIONS

Fuse the interfacing onto the back of each strip of fabric. Round the ends of both strips. On one strip, stitch random rows of decorative patterns from your machine. You may use a marker to diagram the path you want or you can make it up as you go along. Use two or three different colors of thread, possibly including the color of the fabric. Stitch over some decorative cords or yarns to add texture to the design.

Cover the cotton cording in the desired color of piping by cutting a bias strip of fabric wide enough to go around the cording plus ½″ (1.3cm) for the seam allowances. Wrap the bias strip around the cording and stitch next to the cording using a zipper foot or piping foot (Fig. 4-29).

Figure 4-29
Cover the cord to make the piping.

Place the piping around the edges of the embellished strip of fabric with the raw edges even. Place the second strip of fabric face down on top of the embellished strip. With a zipper foot or piping foot, stitch around the edges close to the piping, leaving a 4″ (10cm) opening. Allow ¼″ (6mm) for the seams.

Trim the seams, turn the belt through the opening, and press it. Edgestitch close to the piping, closing the opening as you sew.

Overlap the ends of the belt until it fits comfortably. Stitch the closure tape on the ends and sew the decorative button on the front.

▶ Loop Belt (Fig. 4-30)

This simple belt takes only minutes to make. The loop closure at the front adds interest to any outfit.

Figure 4-30
Loop Belt

MATERIALS NEEDED
2 strips of fabric (1 for the belt and 1 for the lining), each 3″ × 43″ (7.5cm × 109cm) for small to medium sizes or 3″ × 48″ (7.5cm × 122cm) for medium to large sizes

Closure tape, 8″ (20.5cm) of soft side and 3″ (7.5cm) of rough side
Optional: interfacing the same size as the strips of fabric

DIRECTIONS

Fuse interfacing to the back of the strips if the fabric needs extra body.

Stitch the 8″ (20.5cm) of soft side of closure tape on the right side of the lining fabric, 10″ (25.5cm) from the end and centered from top to bottom (Fig. 4-31).

At the same end, on the *right* side of the belt fabric, stitch the 3″ (7.5cm) piece of rough side of the closure tape ¾″ (2cm) from one end, centered from top to bottom.

Place the belt and lining right sides together. Stitch with a ½″ (1.3cm) seam allowance, leaving a 4″ (10cm) opening along one side. Turn right side out and press. Topstitch ¼″ (6mm) from all the edges.

On the end without the closure tape, make a loop by folding 3½″ (9cm) of the strip to the wrong side of the belt and stitching the loop in place (Fig. 4-31).

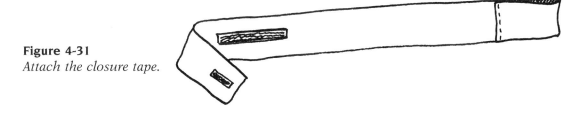

Figure 4-31
Attach the closure tape.

To wear the belt, put the straight end through the loop and pull it tightly. Secure the belt by tucking the loose end under the belt and pressing the two pieces of closure tape together.

Chapter 5
Remnant Sewing

Creating One-of-a-Kind Clothing
with Small Yardages

BUYING FABRICS is a hobby or an avocation for many sewers, and for some of us it can even be an addiction. We love the colors and patterns and textures of all those yards of pieced goods. Most of us have enough yardage to clothe several families, and I've heard just about every excuse, reason, justification, and rationalization for the stashing of all this fabric. My problem is that if I bought yards of every fabric that I wanted, my budget would definitely break under the strain. So when I find a fabric I feel I can't live without, I buy a small piece (a yard or less) or scour the remnant bins until I find a piece at a bargain. This satisfies my need for the fabric but doesn't deplete my pocketbook. The result is that, along with yards of choice material, my fabric stash contains dozens of small pieces of wonderful fabric.

Today's fashion trends lend themselves to using all those small pieces of fabric. Browse through the retail stores and note all of the color-blocked, patchwork, and embellished clothing. The different designs open up limitless possibilities for using remnants that might otherwise go unused.

▶ Color Blocking

DIRECTIONS

Color blocking is probably one of the easiest ways to combine fabrics when putting together a garment with remnants (Fig. 5-1). There are a few considerations to keep in mind when designing a color-blocked project. First, select like or similar-weight fabrics to use together. You may be able to interface the back of one piece to make it comparable to the others, so don't immediately eliminate different weights. The color combination can be any scheme that you choose. Prints and patterns certainly may be used, but they should be kept to a minimum to avoid a cluttered, campy look. Pay attention to the design of the garment pattern, too. Basic designs with only a few pattern pieces work best because they highlight the uniqueness of the color blocking rather than fight the design of the garment for attention.

The simplest blocking method is to take the pattern and cut each piece of the garment from a different color. The color separation lines will simply be the seam lines of the garment. Another way to block the color is to divide one or more of the pattern pieces into a few large pieces. The best way to do this is to piece together the fabrics before you cut out the pattern piece. Piece the fabrics together in a pleasing arrangement to make yardage large enough for the desired pattern piece. After cutting out the entire pattern, stitch the garment together the same as you would if you had used only one kind of fabric.

Figure 5-1
Color-Blocked Blouse

Another method of dividing a design for color blocking is to cut the tissue pattern piece into the sections desired. Remember to add a ½″ (1.3cm) seam allowance to all cut lines to allow for seaming the fabric pieces together.

Yet another option when color blocking a garment is to put sashing between the color separations. These stripes should be of a strong, dominant color that works well with all the other colors you have chosen. Neutrals work nicely, and black is a popular choice because it sets off most colors without overpowering them.

▶ Patchwork Vest (Fig. 5-2)

The green-and-blue vest shown on the cover was made from tapestry and upholstery scraps left over from a home-decorating makeover.

I first learned this technique from Alice Allen, a friend and creative designer who is always coming up with a new twist on classic favorites. It

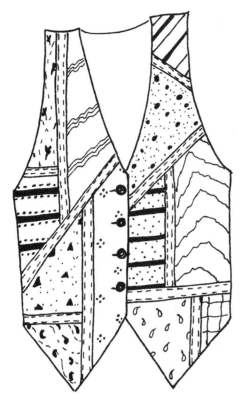

Figure 5-2
Patchwork Vest

has become a favorite of mine, and every vest turns out differently, making each one unique. This design technique also works for jackets, tote bags, and book covers, as well as for many other projects.

MATERIALS NEEDED
Assorted pieces of tapestry and upholstery fabrics
Your favorite vest pattern
1 yard (91.5cm) of 45″-wide (114.5cm) muslin
3–5 yards (2.76m–4.57m) of ⅝″-wide (1.5cm) ribbon
Optional: 3–5 yards (2.76m–4.57m) of trim or cord

DIRECTIONS
Take your favorite vest pattern and trace the outline of the front pattern piece onto muslin. Do this with the right and left sides, making sure to flip the pattern piece so that you don't end up with two left fronts.

When arranging the swatches, work with the right and left sides of the vest at the same time to make sure the design of the swatches remains balanced and flows well across the front of the garment. Start with one of the larger swatches and pin it in place on the muslin near the center front of the vest. Then work your way out as you place the remaining fabrics. Take a second swatch of fabric and place it next to the first swatch with the raw edges slightly overlapping.

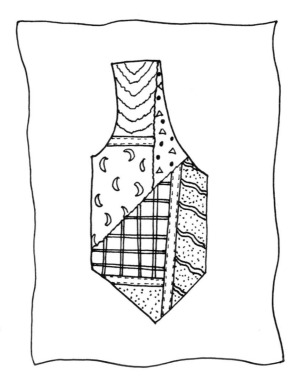

Figure 5-3
The designed vest front

Pay attention to the balance of the design, looking at such things as the placement of colors, the distribution of prints, and the evenness of textures. Don't put all the dark colors together or all the printed fabrics together unless you have other fabric pieces with strong characteristics that will balance the design as a whole. For instance, if you plan to add numerous trinkets and buttons on one side as extra embellishments, you might want to arrange stronger colors and prints on the other side.

Continue placing swatches until you have covered the front of the vest with fabric. Trim away any excess fabric to make the swatches fit together. Keep in mind the marked outline of the vest, even though you may have already covered it with fabric. As you decide on the placement of the swatches, trim them to fit the drawn outline (Fig. 5-3). After you have arranged the swatches, pin or baste them in place and finish trimming around the outside edges of the pattern piece. You may want to place the pattern tissue over the fabric to double-check the cutting lines.

For the dividing strips, use ribbon or a bias strip of fabric folded under on both long edges. Center the strip over each intersection where the fabrics meet and edgestitch it in place, making sure to cover all the raw edges of the fabric. By slightly overlapping the edges of the swatches, you eliminate the risk of the fabric pulling away from the ribbon at a later time. If the ribbon comes to an end somewhere in the middle of the garment rather than in the seam allowance, simply fold under the edge and stitch across it to secure it. Plan the order in which you stitch the ribbon, covering the short edges first, so that a longer length will cover the end of the previous one. One of the fun things about this method of design is that it constantly changes as you work with it. Stop and look as you stitch the ribbons in place. You may find yourself rearranging and making changes as you go along.

For extra texture and emphasis, couch a trim down the center of the ribbon. On the upholstery vest shown, I used a rayon braid the same color as the ribbon. With nylon thread and a zigzag stitch, I applied the braid on top of the ribbon after doing the edgestitching.

Sew the vest together following your pattern directions, or try the method that I find easiest and quickest with absolutely no hand sewing.

Vest Quick-Finish Method

To finish the vest, stitch the vest front and back together at the shoulders. Do the same with the lining front and back.

With right sides together, stitch the vest and lining together around all of the edges *except the side seams (there are four) and the center-back lower edge,* where you should leave a 4"–5" (10cm–12.5cm) opening, as shown in Figure 5-4.

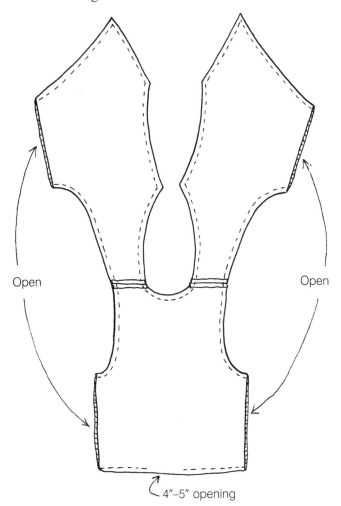

Open   Open

Figure 5-4
Stitch the vest and lining together, right sides facing.

4"–5" opening

Clip the seam allowances on the curves, turn the vest through the bottom opening, and press it.

Reach into the lower back opening and pull out the vest and lining front and back portions of one side of the vest. Place the right sides together (lining to lining and vest to vest) and stitch along the seams, forming a complete circle (Fig. 5-5). This will stitch both the vest and lining side seams. Smooth this side out, allowing it to take its finished shape, and then repeat the whole process on the other side of the vest.

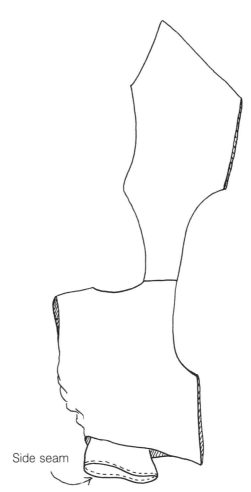

Figure 5-5
Stitch the side seams of the lining and the vest.

Side seam

Edgestitch all the edges of the vest, closing the lower back opening as you sew.

Add the finishing touches by embellishing the vest with trinkets. You can recycle buttons from your button jar or unused baubles in your jewelry box for this task. Be sure to choose items that will enhance the design you've created. Another fun way to design patchwork vests is to select a theme. Choose anything from a seasonal theme (Christmas, for example) to a period theme (perhaps Victoriana) and allow your imagination to run free.

► Signature Vest

DIRECTIONS

The blue and pink vest shown in the Color Section was put together in the same way as the Patchwork Vest in this chapter. If you look closely, you'll see that many of the swatches in this vest have been decorated with techniques and stitches done on the sewing machine. Create your own personal statement by using your favorite embellishments and trying out some of those little-used decorative stitches on your machine. This is a great project that allows you to play with your sewing machine and become familiar with more of its functions.

All of the embellishments I chose were done on swatches of fabric before the vest was designed. Use interfacing or stabilizer wherever necessary to keep the fabric from pulling or puckering. Some of my favorite embellishments used on the vest shown are described in detail below.

Machine-Embroidered Flowers

The bouquet of flowers on the upper-left front of the Signature Vest in the Color Section is a machine-embroidery project that even a beginning stitcher can do.

With a fabric marker, draw a bouquet of flowers by sketching the stems and placing a dot at the center of each flower (Fig. 5-6).

Figure 5-6
Machine-embroidered flowers

Using embroidery thread, stitch the stems with a reinforced straight stitch. If your machine does not have a reinforced stitch, stitch the stems two or three times using a normal straight stitch to give them a heavier look.

For the flowers, set the machine on its widest zigzag stitch. Drop or cover the feed dogs so that the fabric will not move as you stitch. At the dot marking the center of a flower, stitch back and forth over the same spot about 6–9 times to form a bartack. End with the needle in the fabric at the marked dot. Lift the foot and pivot with the needle in the fabric. Make another bartack, ending with the needle at the center of the fabric. Continue pivoting and making bartacks until you complete a circle, coming back to where you started. To give the flower a more natural look, add an odd number of petals. Using a variegated or multicolored embroidery thread will give a pretty change of color to the flowers and add depth and richness to the stitching.

Twisted Tucks (Fig. 5-7)

Sew a series of evenly spaced narrow tucks across the swatch of fabric. Next, stitch parallel rows of any stitch (straight or decorative) across the tucks, alternating the direction so that the tucks twist in opposite ways.

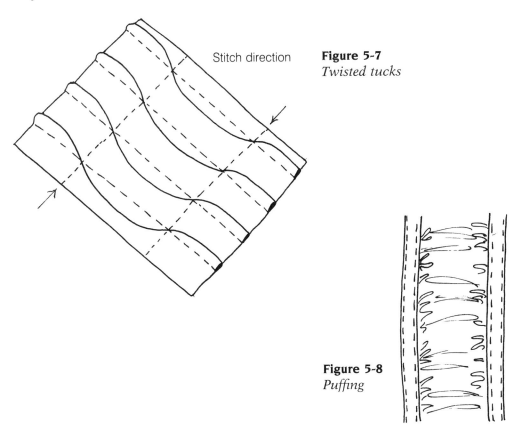

Stitch direction

Figure 5-7
Twisted tucks

Figure 5-8
Puffing

Puffing (Fig. 5-8)

Puffing is a technique used in French hand sewing. Usually done on a strip of fine batiste fabric, the puffing is gathered on each side and stitched to *entredeux*. The variation shown on this vest uses a cotton print. Use any lightweight fabric and cut a strip twice as long as the finished length desired. The width used on the vest shown was 3″ (7.5cm). After cutting the strip, stitch a gathering thread ¼″ (6mm) from each long edge. Pull up the gathering thread until you achieve the desired length. As you place the gathered strips on the front of the vest, evenly distribute the gathers across the strip of fabric.

Texturized Fabric (Fig. 5-9)

The swatch shown at the middle of the right side of the vest is a cotton fabric stitched to add texture to the surface. The trick is to use regular sewing thread in the needle and elastic thread in the bobbin so

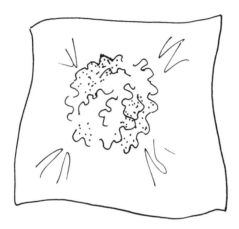

Figure 5-9
Texturized fabric

that the stitching pulls up the fabric to create a textured surface. Place the fabric in a hoop to hold it taut while stitching. Use a straight or zigzag stitch to make random patterns. When you remove the hoop, the fabric will pull up and texturize the surface. Keep the stitching (texture) away from the edges so that the swatch will lie flat as you sew the vest front.

When designing the front of the vest, combine the decorated swatches with some plain ones. The blue pieces at the center front of the vest shown was an upholstery swatch from a discarded sample book.

Use a coordinating fabric for the back and lining of the vest. The fabric could be an actual lining fabric or a light- to medium-weight fabric that blends well with the patches.

▶ Remnant Jacket (Fig. 5-10)

DIRECTIONS

Stitching remnants together for a project is a fun exercise in creativity. As you sort through your fabric stash, look for pieces of fabrics that are larger than swatches. I consider a remnant to be a piece that measures between ½ (45.5cm) and 1 yard (91.5cm). You'll be amazed at how

Figure 5-10
Remnant Jacket

many of your fabrics will coordinate and look great together. Most people are drawn to the same types and color families of fabrics, so you are automatically coordinating pieces each time you buy.

The jacket shown in the Color Section was made from beautiful remnants of expensive fabrics. I found the fabrics in an exclusive fabric shop on a table advertising 75% off the remnant price. They range in price from $15 to $45 a yard. I put the entire jacket together for less than $15.

You can blend the fabrics by using some embellishment and sewing machine techniques to make the design more interesting and to pull the look together. Some techniques that work well in this capacity are decorative stitching, quilting, and couching.

Decorative Stitching

Decorative stitching is a great way to add color and pattern to a fabric that either looks dull or just doesn't go with the other fabrics as much as you'd like (Fig. 5-11). Pull some colors or designs from the other fabrics and re-create them on the drab piece. You may need to use a stabilizer on the wrong side to keep the fabric flat and to prevent puckering as you stitch.

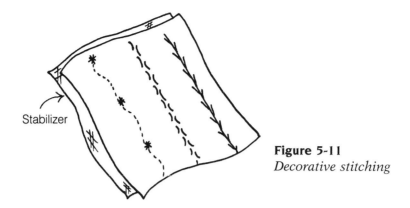

Figure 5-11
Decorative stitching

Quilting

Quilting can add weight and texture to a swatch of fabric (Fig. 5-12). If you choose several prints or embellished fabrics, you may decide it's distracting to have only one solid, smooth piece of fabric in the midst of the design. Eliminate this distraction while preserving the solidity of the piece by backing the piece with fleece and quilting the surface. Use either

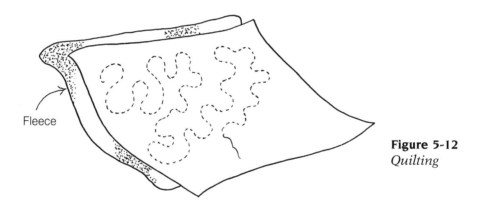

Figure 5-12
Quilting

simple channel quilting in parallel lines or a more intricate design done with the feed dogs lowered. You might choose to duplicate the shape of the motif in one of the printed fabrics.

Couching

Couching is a term borrowed from hand embroidery that means "stitching over cord." The finished look of this technique can be as different as night and day, depending on your choice of cord, thread, and stitch (Fig. 5-13). You might choose rattail cord, soutache braid, heavy decorative thread, yarns, or narrow ribbons. Almost any stitch can be used over the top of the cord. If you want to highlight the cord, use nylon

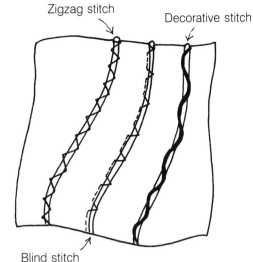

Zigzag stitch

Decorative stitch

Figure 5-13
Couching stitches

Blind stitch

thread with a blind stitch or zigzag. The stitch then becomes invisible and allows the decorative cord to show through. Matching the color of the needle thread with the background fabric will make it appear as if the cord is woven into the fabric. When couching, remember to use stabilizer or interfacing to provide a strong foundation on which to stitch the cord.

Use a commercial pattern that has few pieces and a simple, un-constructed design. Cut the jacket out of a base fabric, such as muslin or lightweight cotton. Position the remnants in a pleasing arrangement on top of the fabric base. Then seam the pieces together, trimming the swatches if necessary. Position the pattern piece on the seamed fabrics and trim close to the pattern where needed. Sew the jacket together according to the pattern instructions.

Chapter 6
The Second Time Around

Reusing Denim, Ultrasuede,
and Men's Ties

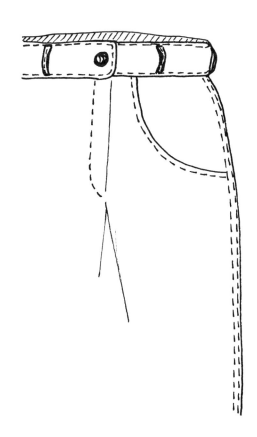

SOME FABRICS are delicate and must be handled carefully in order to get even a limited amount of wear from them. Others wear like iron. Two of the latter, denim and Ultrasuede, seem to last forever and lend themselves to a variety of projects. The following pages offer a number of ways to recycle these versatile fabrics into useful and practical items.

DENIM

Denim has long been an American favorite. Used for work clothes since the 1800s because of its durability, denim is now used in all areas of fashion, from baby clothes to evening dresses.

The most common use for denim is still jeans, and most people own several pairs. Finding old, discarded jeans to use for projects never seems to be a problem. The thrift shops and secondhand stores are full of jeans that contain yards of serviceable denim. For a small amount of money, you can purchase denim in all weights and shades of blue for a variety of projects. Ask your friends to donate their used and worn-out jeans to your cause and you'll have more than you need. In fact, the only problem with finding old jeans is that it is sometimes hard to tell worn jeans from the new pricey ones with designer holes in them.

▶ Back-Pocket Organizer (Fig. 6-1)

Use discarded jeans to make this unique jewelry and scarf organizer (pictured on the cover and in the Color Section). Hang it on the wall to hold all your fashion accessories.

MATERIALS NEEDED
Medium-weight, firmly woven fabric for backing, 24″ × 36″ (61cm × 91.5cm)
Several pairs of discarded jeans with patch pockets and belt loops
Small pieces of plastic canvas
Small curtain rod or dowel

DIRECTIONS
Cut off the pockets from the jeans. There is no need to remove any stitching; simply trim the back portion of the jeans away from the pocket so that you have only the pocket front left.

Cut the back waist area from one pair of jeans and remove several belt loops from another pair.

Cut the legs of the jeans into strips of any length and width. Seam these strips together to make a piece of fabric 24″ × 36″ (61cm × 91.5cm) as shown in Figure 6-2.

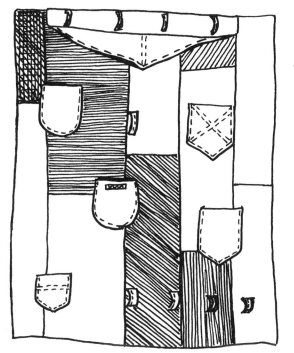

Figure 6-1
Back-Pocket Organizer

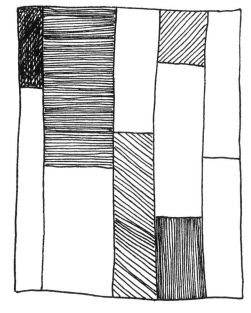

Figure 6-2
Fabric pieced from jeans

Place the denim and backing fabric right sides together. Stitch around all the edges using a ½″ (1.3cm) seam allowance and leaving a 4″ (10cm) opening for turning. Trim the corners, turn the piece right side out, and press it. Edgestitch all the edges and close the opening.

Place the back waist piece at the center top of the fabric and topstitch it in place. Topstitch the pockets on in a random pattern, leaving their top edge open. Position the belt loops in various places around pockets.

To hang the organizer, stitch three belt loops across the top edge on the back side. Position these loops 1″ to 1½″ (2.5cm to 4cm) down from the top edge. Slip a small curtain rod or dowel through the loops and hang the organizer on the wall (Fig. 6-3).

Cut pieces of plastic canvas to fit a few of the pockets. Attach earrings to the canvas to keep them together in pairs before placing them in the pocket. Slip scarves, belts, and necklaces through the loops. Make another organizer for your sewing room to hold small supplies and miscellaneous notions.

Figure 6-3
Hanging the organizer

▶ Patch Pocket Coin Purse (Fig. 6-4)

If you have patch pockets left over, you can make this easy coin purse.

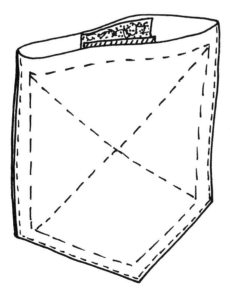

Figure 6-4
Patch Pocket Coin Purse

MATERIALS NEEDED
2 patch pockets of the same size and shape
Paper-backed fusible web
Medium-weight fabric for the lining
3″–4″ (7.5cm × 10cm) of ½″ (1.3cm) closure tape

DIRECTIONS

Remove the pockets from the jeans as you did for the Back-Pocket Organizer. Trim away any excess fabric from around the pockets.

Cut a piece of fabric for the lining of the purse by tracing around the pocket and adding ¼″ (6mm) around all the edges. Cut out two pieces of lining. Fold under ¼″ (6mm) around all the edges and press.

Iron the paper-backed fusible web to the back of the lining fabric.

Peel off the paper and fuse the wrong side of the lining to the wrong side of the pocket (Fig. 6-5). Repeat with the second pocket and lining piece.

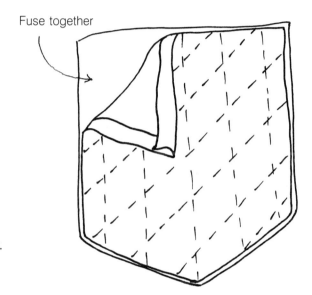

Figure 6-5
Fuse the lining to the pocket.

On the upper edge of the lining side, stitch one side of the closure tape to each pocket.

Place the pockets wrong sides together and topstitch around them from the upper-right edge to the upper-left edge. Use a reinforced stitch or stitch around twice for added security.

Fill the pocket purse with money and go shopping!

▶ Chenille and Denim Bathrobe (Fig. 6-6)

This comfy bathrobe (shown on the back cover) was made from an old chenille bedspread that was thin in several places but was still in good condition. The facing and trim came from a favorite soft denim skirt that was worn for more than eight years but finally was torn so badly that it couldn't be repaired.

This "one size fits most" robe is made from rectangles of fabric, so if you need to alter it to fit, you can simply enlarge or reduce the size of the

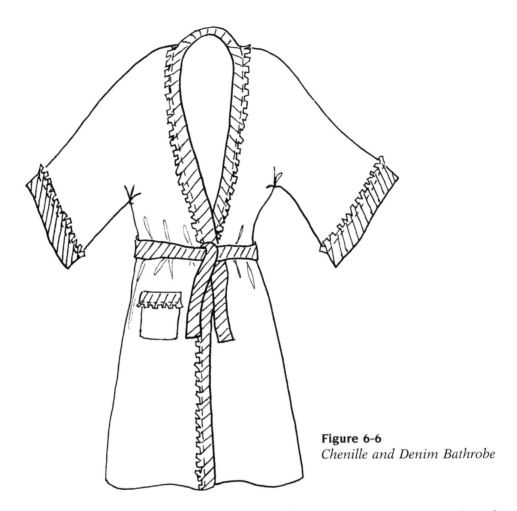

Figure 6-6
Chenille and Denim Bathrobe

rectangles. The robe goes together quickly, so you can cut it out this afternoon and snuggle up in it this evening.

The trim is denim turned to the outside of the robe, topstitched, and clipped to make a textured edge that will fray a little more every time you wash the robe.

MATERIALS NEEDED

Outer fabric, such as chenille, flannel, or terry cloth. You will need enough to cut the following rectangles:

Back—28″ × 40″ (71cm × 101.5cm)
Front—two 14″ × 40″ (35.5cm × 101.5cm)
Sleeves—two 24″ × 10″ (71cm × 25.5cm)
Pocket—7½″ × 8″ (19.5cm × 20.5cm)

Denim needed for the reverse facing, which also serves as the trim: (If necessary, you can piece the strips of denim together to make the sizes you need. When piecing the fabric, stitch the strips together at a 45-degree angle to make the joining less conspicuous.)

Front opening—two strips, 2″ × 47″ (5cm × 119.5cm)
Sleeves—two strips 2″ × 24″ (5cm × 61cm)
Pocket—one strip, 2″ × 7½″ (5cm × 19.5cm)
Belt—one strip 2½″ × 60″ (6.5cm × 152.5cm), or as long as
   you wish

DIRECTIONS

Pocket

Place the right side of the denim facing to the wrong side of the
pocket on the 7½″ (19.5cm) side. Stitch, using a ½″ (1.3cm) seam allowance. Fold the facing to the right side of the pocket and press the pocket
so that the facing seam forms the top edge.

Topstitch 1″ (2.5cm) from the top edge of the pocket through the
denim. Clip the raw edge of the denim every ½″ (1.3cm).

Press under ½″ (1.3cm) on all remaining sides.

Position the pocket 11″ (28cm) up from the lower edge and 3″ (7.5cm)
from the edge of the *right* side. Topstitch it in place.

Robe Body

Shape the back neck edge by measuring 1″ (2.5cm) at the center back.
Mark 11½″ (29.5cm) in from each side edge (Fig. 6-7). Draw a semicircle
connecting the three marks and trim on that line.

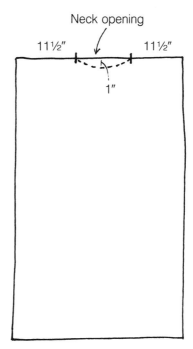

Figure 6-7
Shape the back neck edge.

To shape the front neck edge, measure 12″ (30.5cm) down at the center front on both rectangles (Fig. 6-8). Measure 1″ (2.5cm) in at the top neck edge and mark. Draw a line to connect the two marks on each side of the front. Trim on this line.

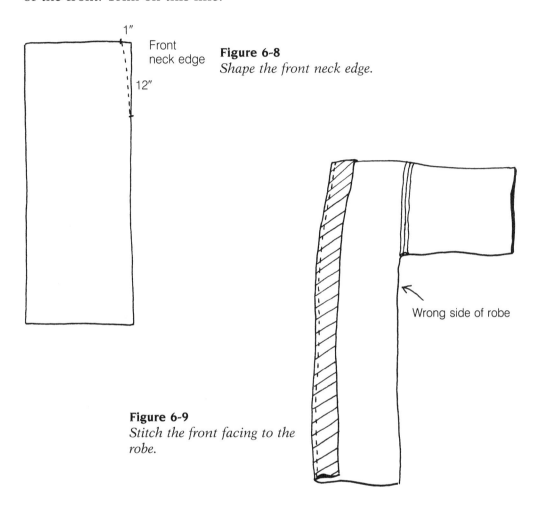

1″

Front neck edge

12″

Figure 6-8
Shape the front neck edge.

Wrong side of robe

Figure 6-9
Stitch the front facing to the robe.

With right sides together, stitch the fronts to the back at the shoulder seam, using a ½″ (1.3cm) seam allowance. Use a serger stitch or a zigzag stitch to finish the edges of the seam.

Stitch the two denim front-opening strips together across the 2″ (5cm) side, using a ½″ (1.3cm) seam allowance. Place the facing strip with the right side of the strip to the wrong side of the robe opening and neck edge. With a ½″ (1.3cm) seam allowance, straight stitch from the right lower edge to the left lower edge (Fig. 6-9).

Fold the facing forward to the front of the robe. Press and pin it in place. Stitch 1″ (2.5cm) from the finished opening edge, leaving the raw edges of the trim exposed (Fig. 6-10).

Clip the raw edges of the trim every ½″ (1.3cm). When you wash the robe, these edges will fray and curl.

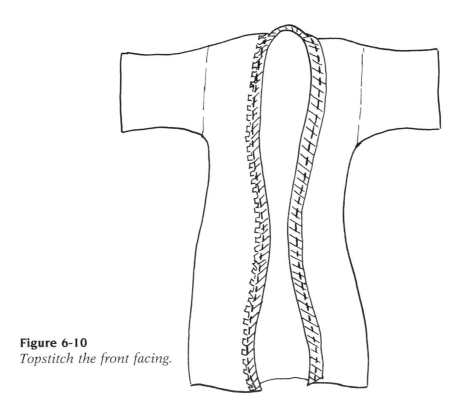

Figure 6-10
Topstitch the front facing.

Sleeves

Mark the center of the top sleeve edge (the 24½″ [62.5cm] side). With the right sides together, pin the sleeve to the body of the robe, matching the center of the sleeve to the shoulder seam. Stitch, using a ½″ (1.3cm) seam allowance.

With the right side of the sleeve facing next to the wrong side of the sleeve bottom edge, straight stitch using a ½″ (1.3cm) seam allowance.

Open out the facing and fold the robe right sides together. Stitch the underarm and side seams.

Fold the facing to the right side and press. Stitch 1″ (2.5cm) from the finished edge.

Clip the raw edge of the facing/trim every ½″ (1.3cm).

Turn up the lower edge of the robe ¼″ (6mm) and then another 1″ (2.5cm) for the hem. Stitch in place.

Belt

Fold the denim strip right sides together and stitch, using a ¼″ (6mm) seam allowance and leaving a 4″ (10cm) opening. Turn the strip right side out and press it. Edgestitch around all the edges, closing the opening as you sew. (The belt should be soft and flexible for tying, so you do not need interfacing.)

ULTRASUEDE PATCHWORK

A synthetic fabric, Ultrasuede has a unique position in recycling. It is a petroleum product, so the process of manufacturing it uses up one of our nonrenewable resources. But because it is polyurethane, it rarely wears out and can be used over and over again. I've seen Ultrasuede garments that were sewn 15–20 years ago. After being taken apart and restyled, they looked like new garments. If you happen to come across an out-of-style Ultrasuede garment, use it to create a new, up-to-date, luxurious addition to your closet.

If you don't have an entire garment to work with, choose a few small pieces left over from other projects. You can piece together tiny slivers of Ultrasuede to build larger pieces of fabric for some great projects. Start with a piece of Ultrasuede that has at least one straight edge. Take a second piece with a straight edge and overlap the edges slightly (about 1/16″ or 1mm). Using nylon thread and a medium zigzag stitch, sew the two pieces together. Guide the fabric so that the stitch is centered over the edge of the fabric on top. The pieces must lie perfectly flat, so let them relax as you sew. If the overlap becomes more than 1/16″ (1mm), trim the excess from the wrong side after you stitch.

After stitching, use a rotary cutter to straighten the outer edge formed by the first two pieces. Zigzag a third piece to this edge. Continue adding pieces of Ultrasuede until you have a swatch of fabric large enough for the project you've chosen (Fig. 6-11).

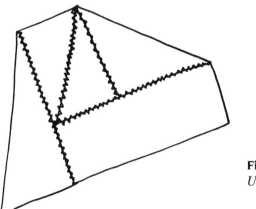

Figure 6-11
Ultrasuede patchwork

There are two important things to remember when making Ultrasuede patchwork: (1) trim the edges as straight as possible, and (2) let the fabric lie perfectly flat as you work. Using a walking foot or an even feed foot will help feed the fabric easily and keep it flat.

▶ Paperback Book Cover with Bookmark (Fig. 6-12)

Book covers are quick and easy to make with some odds and ends of Ultrasuede. They'll dress up that paperback book you're reading and protect it when you throw it into your purse or tote bag. Complete it with a fabric bookmark to keep your place.

Figure 6-12
Paperback Book Cover with
Bookmark

MATERIALS NEEDED

8″ × 10″ (20.5cm × 25.5cm) piece of Ultrasuede, pieced together as described earlier in this chapter, which will be trimmed and squared to 7½″ × 9½″ (19.5cm × 24.5cm) [These directions are for a 1″-thick (2.5cm) book. To make a cover for a thicker book, add the appropriate amount to the width (9½″; 24.5cm) of the rectangle.]

7½″ × 9½″ (19.5cm × 24.5cm) piece of Ultrasuede (or sized to match your patchwork piece)

2 pieces of Ultrasuede, 3″ × 7½″ (7.5cm × 19.5cm) each

A strip of Ultrasuede, ½″ × 10″ (1.3cm × 25.5cm) for the bookmark

7½″ × 9½″ (19.5cm × 24.5cm) piece of fusible web (or sized to match your patchwork piece)

Glue stick

DIRECTIONS

Fuse the web to the back of the patchwork piece. Set your iron on the wool setting and use a press cloth to protect the nap of the Ultrasuede.

Peel the paper from the web and fuse the patchwork to the corresponding solid piece with *wrong sides together*.

Place a short edge of the bookmark at the top of the center front with right sides together. Use a glue stick to baste the strip in place.

Place 3″ (7.5cm) pieces on the *inside* of the book cover so that their right sides face up. Position one on each end with the outside edges even.

Using a straight or decorative stitch, sew around all the edges of the book cover, stitching the flaps and bookmark in place (Fig. 6-13).

Slip the cover of the paperback book under each flap.

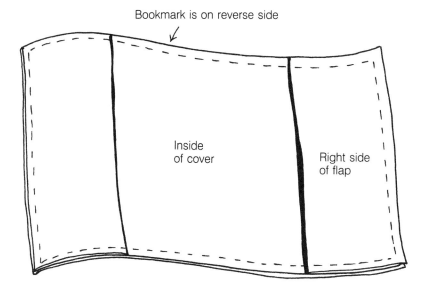

Bookmark is on reverse side

Inside of cover

Right side of flap

Figure 6-13
Stitch all the way around the cover.

TIE IT UP!

Another source of fabric that seems to be long-lasting and plentiful is men's ties—those beautiful, colorful strips of fabric that can be used for all types of projects, from quilts to skirts (Fig. 6-14). Open up the tie by

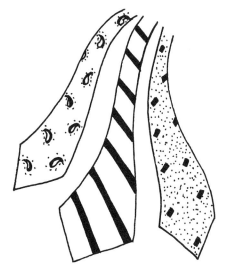

Figure 6-14
Ties, ties, ties!

removing the stitching from the back and lightly press it flat. The next step is to decide whether you want to use the fabric in strips or patches, then cut the fabric accordingly.

The beautiful tie vest shown in the Color Section was designed by Kathy Embry of the marketing department at Bernina of America. It was pieced and stitched using the patchwork method described in Chapter 5. Take a close look and notice that not only was the fabric used in small pieces, but the labels were used as embellishments after the front was designed and assembled. What a great way to use up those lovely ties that have gone out of style!

The dividing strips on the vest were made by stitching various ribbons and trims, instead of using only one color of ribbon, as was done on the other vests shown. This is another great way to use up those odds and ends of trim left over from other projects. The closures used on this vest are fur hooks given to the designer by her grandmother. So don't overlook some choices that may not seem obvious at first. Rummage through those sewing boxes.

Chapter 7
Home Sewing

Sewing Pillows and
Duvet Covers

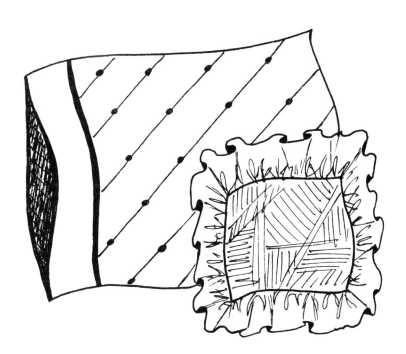

SEWING FOR your home is a satisfying way to express your creativity and save money at the same time. Custom treatments for the home are expensive, so making them yourself can definitely be a bargain—and even more so if you use recycled fabrics and materials.

▶ Crazy Patchwork Pillow (Fig. 7-1)

When sewing for the home, why not make a project that will pull together all the patterns, prints, and textures that you spent weeks selecting and coordinating? Making throw pillows in crazy patchwork designs will let you use small leftover pieces and echo the theme you have chosen for a particular room.

Figure 7-1
Crazy Patchwork Pillow

Crazy patchwork can be worked in a number of ways, and while the process of making the patches may seem random, it does take some thought, imagination, and planning. The following directions are for the 14″-square (35.5cm) pillow shown in the Color Section.

MATERIALS NEEDED
A 16″-square (40.5cm) piece of light- to medium-weight base fabric. (This fabric will not show, so take this opportunity to make use of those out-of-style or "Why did I buy this?" fabrics taking up space in your stash.)
Small odds and ends of remnants and pieces of fabric used to decorate the room for which the pillow is being made
Buttons, trinkets, and decorative threads

2 pieces of backing fabric, 10″ × 16″ (25.5cm × 40.5cm) each
A 6″ × 72″ (15cm × 183cm) strip of fabric for the ruffle
5″–6″ (12.5cm–15cm) of closure tape
Optional: 2 yards (1.84m) of 1½″-wide (4cm) lace for the second
   ruffle

DIRECTIONS

The easiest way that I have found to start crazy patchwork is to begin in the center of the base fabric. Cut a swatch of fabric so that it has at least five sides. This will make your patchwork look more random and help you avoid a straight geometric result. Pin the swatch in place in the center of the base fabric.

Beginning on any side, place a second swatch next to the first piece, right side down. Using a ¼″ (6mm) seam allowance, stitch along one edge of the swatch, stitching through both pieces and the base fabric (Fig. 7-2).

Flip the second fabric over so that the right side is up, then press.

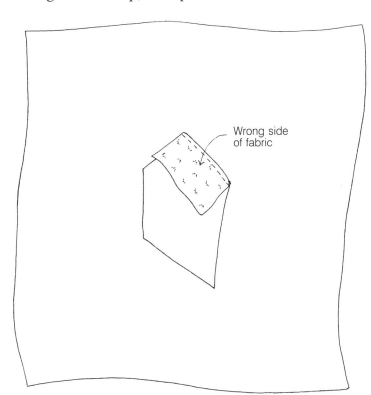

Wrong side
of fabric

Figure 7-2
Crazy patchwork, step #1

Stitch a third piece to the first two, covering an edge on both (Fig. 7-3). Trim away any excess fabric.

Flip the third fabric over so that the right side is up, then press.

Continue this method, working from the center out to the edges, all the way around (Fig. 7-4). It is best to work in one direction (either clockwise or counterclockwise) once you have started.

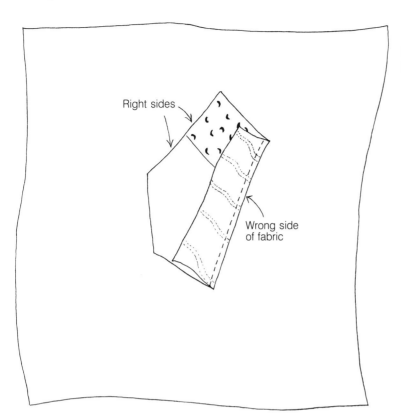

Figure 7-3
Crazy patchwork, step #2

Figure 7-4
Crazy patchwork, step #3

If your swatches are not large enough for the outer edge pieces, stitch together several small pieces and attach this piece to the base fabric.

Once you have completed the patchwork, embellish it by sewing decorative machine stitches over the intersections where the patches meet. Add decorative buttons and trinkets to give the pillow a Victorian look, but don't attach them too close to the seam allowances. Lace and trim can also be added as embellishment.

After decorating the crazy patchwork fabric, cut it into a 16″ (35.5cm) square and proceed with the following directions.

Hem one 10″ (25.5cm) side on each of the backing pieces by folding under ¼″ (6mm) and then 1″ (2.5cm). Topstitch the hem and overlap the hemmed edges of the two pieces. Stitch the closure tape on the hemmed edges to hold the two together.

Overlap the hemmed edges 1″ (2.5cm) and trim the backing to the same size as the pieced front.

Fold the ruffle strip in half lengthwise, wrong sides together, and press it. (If you want to add a lace ruffle, place it on top of the folded fabric ruffle with the raw edges even.)

Gather the ruffle fabric along the raw edges by zigzagging over a cord. Pull the cord up and distribute the gathers evenly around the right side of the front of the pillow, with the raw edges of the ruffle even with the raw edge of the pillow (Fig. 7-5).

Place the front and back right sides together and stitch, using a ½″ (1.3cm) seam allowance. Trim the corners and turn through the opening in the back.

Insert the pillow form through the back opening. (See Recycling Idea #4 in Chapter 1 to learn how to make your own pillow form.)

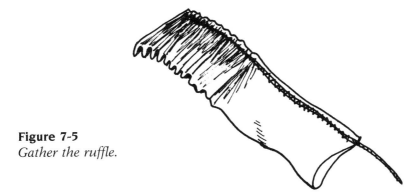

Figure 7-5
Gather the ruffle.

▶ Piped and Pieced Pillow (Fig. 7-6)

Another way to use small pieces of fabric to make a pillow is to piece the top and use piping as a divider between the strips. Again, you will

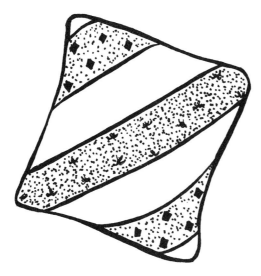

Figure 7-6
Piped and Pieced Pillow

build on a base fabric, but this time you will add a thin layer of fleece or batting on top of it. The pillow is actually pieced and quilted at the same time.

MATERIALS NEEDED

13″ (33cm) square of pieced and quilted fabric (see directions that follow)
14½″ (37cm) square of backing fabric, cut in half
Piping (covered cording)
12″–15″ (30.5cm–38cm) of closure tape
12″ (30.5cm) pillow form

DIRECTIONS

Place the fleece or batting on top of the base fabric. Starting in the center, pin one strip of fabric in place. The strips must be long enough to go across the block and cover the edges of the pillow foundation.

Place the piping (covered cord) along one edge of the first strip with the raw edges even. Put the next strip on top of the piping with the right side down and the raw edges even. Stitch close to the piping using a zipper foot or piping foot (Fig. 7-7). Flip over and press. Continue working in a diagonal pattern until you reach the corner. Then work your way out to the other corner, placing piping in each seam line, until you have covered the base fabric. Trim the pieced fabric to the desired size.

To make the pillow pictured in the Color Section and on the back cover, use the following directions.

Pin piping around the edges of the pieced pillow top with the raw edges even. Clip the seam allowance of the piping at each corner so that the piping will turn smoothly. Stitch close to the cord using a zipper foot or cording foot.

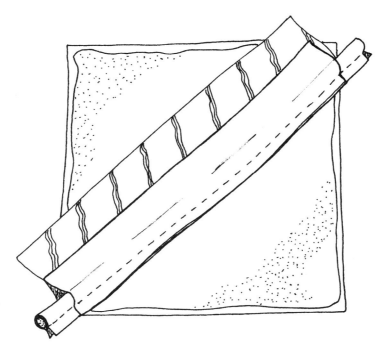

Figure 7-7
Piece the pillow top.

Hem one side on each of the backing pieces by folding under ¼″ (6mm) and then 1″ (2.5cm). Topstitch the hem and overlap the hemmed edges of the two pieces (Fig. 7-8). Stitch closure tape on the hemmed edges to hold the two together.

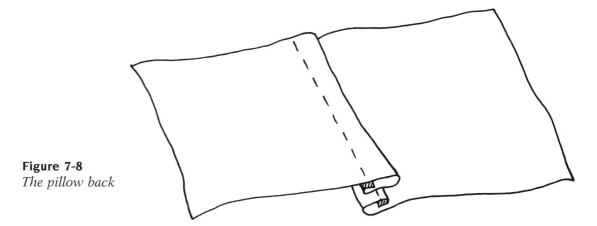

Figure 7-8
The pillow back

Overlap the hemmed edges and secure them with the closure tape. If needed, trim the backing to the same size as the front.

Place the front and back of the pillow right sides together. Sew around all the edges, using a ¼″ (6mm) seam allowance and stitching close to the piping. Trim the seams and turn through the opening in the back.

Insert a 12″ (30.5cm) pillow form through the opening. (See Recycling Idea #4 in Chapter 1 on how to make your own pillow form.) Plump out the corners by stuffing them with loose fiberfill.

▶ Duvet Cover

Does your bedroom need a decorating lift? You can easily change the look and the feel of the room without completely replacing all of the bedclothes. Making a duvet cover will allow you to change your color scheme or let you use a comforter that is worn out.

You can use fabric for the duvet cover or make it quick and easy by using designer sheets.

MATERIALS NEEDED
1 comforter
2 sheets slightly larger than the comforter
18″ (45.5cm) of closure tape

DIRECTIONS
Measure the comforter and add 1″ (2.5cm) to all four sides. This is the size needed for the front of the cover. Cut one of the sheets to this size.

For the back, add 1″ (2.5cm) to the width of the comforter and 3″ (7.5cm) to the length. Divide the back length measurement into thirds and cut one piece of sheet to equal one-third of the total measurement. The other piece should equal the remaining two-thirds. Cut these pieces from each end of the sheet so that the hem of the sheet will create the finished edges of the backing opening (Fig. 7-9).

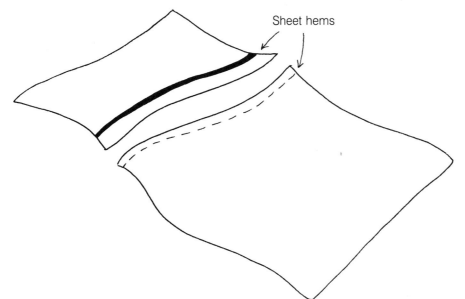

Sheet hems

Figure 7-9
Cut the duvet cover from sheets.

Cut the closure tape into three equal pieces and position them evenly across the hemmed edge of the back pieces (Fig. 7-10). The edges of sheet should overlap 2″ (5cm).

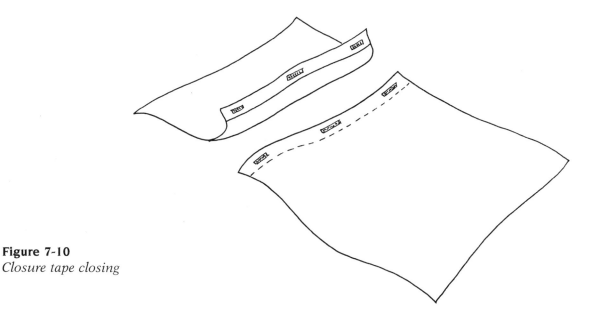

Figure 7-10
Closure tape closing

Place the front and back pieces right sides together and stitch or serge around all four sides, using a ½″ (1.3cm) seam allowance (Fig. 7-11). The cover should be the same size as the comforter so that the comforter fits snugly inside. Turn the cover through the opening on the back side.

Insert the comforter through the opening in the back of the cover.

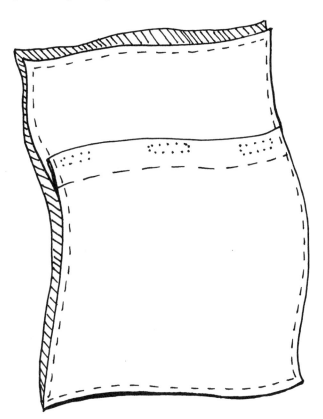

Figure 7-11
Stitch the seams of the Duvet Cover.

Chapter 8
The Button Box

*Embellishing and Decorating
with Buttons*

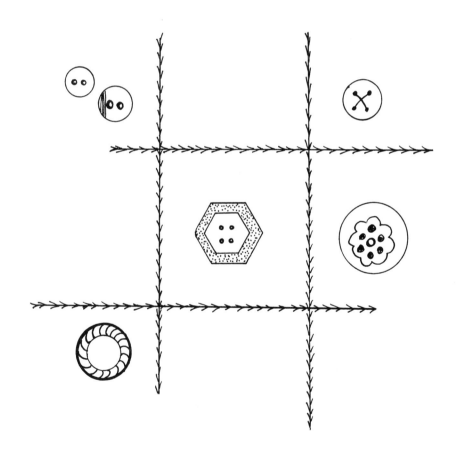

BUTTONS SEEM to collect and multiply faster than we can use them. How many times has a pattern called for three buttons and the ones you want come only on a card of four? One more contribution for the button box! Then there are the extra buttons that come with ready-to-wear garments "just in case." It doesn't take long to accumulate a generous collection of odd-sized, odd-shaped trinkets in your button box. The box becomes a treasury of color, shape, sparkle, and texture. The advantage of having a button box is that you always have just the button you need for a particular project, but buttons can be used for more than just holding clothes together. They're also great for decoration, embellishment, and trimming.

▶ Button-Bolstered Vests

DIRECTIONS

The button-embellished vest shown in the Color Section was made from a perfectly serviceable vest that needed a lift. It hadn't been worn in several years and it needed to be "dressed up" a bit to be current. I began by raiding my button box and came up with a varied selection to adorn the vest. After laying the vest out flat, I arranged and rearranged the buttons until I found a pleasing design. Using a fabric marker, I marked where I wanted to place the buttons on the vest. After basting the smaller, flat buttons on the vest using a glue stick, I removed the larger ones and put them on a tabletop in the general order that I had placed them on the

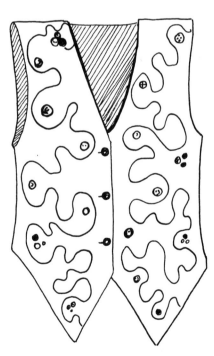

Figure 8-1
Button-Embellished Man's Vest

vest. The next step was to sew them onto the vest. Using dental floss or three strands of embroidery floss will help ensure that the buttons will remain firmly attached for the life of the garment. You may be able to sew on some of the buttons with your machine. Check your owner's manual for specific directions.

Decorating a man's discarded vest with some unusual decorative buttons is another way to create a beautiful addition to your wardrobe to dress up jeans or slacks (Fig. 8-1). Begin by laying out the vest and placing your selection of buttons in a random pattern across the front of the vest. Once you have found a pleasing arrangement, stitch the buttons in place. Use fabric paint or embroidery stitches to decorate around the buttons and pull the design together.

▶ Button Collar Brooch (Fig. 8-2)

Buttons also make wonderful trinkets for fashioning one-of-a-kind pieces of jewelry, such as this collar brooch. The collar brooch begins as a small piece of cloth that fits under the collar of a blouse and shows only at the front of the neck. Embellished with a variety of buttons, it becomes a jewel piece to dress up a plain shirt or blouse.

Figure 8-2
Button Collar Brooch

MATERIALS NEEDED
16″ (40.5cm) square of medium-weight fabric
Lightweight fusible interfacing
Assorted buttons and trinkets
Closure tape

DIRECTIONS
Cut two of the pattern pieces shown in Figure 8-3 and interface each with lightweight fusible interfacing.

Stitch the pieces together, right sides facing, using a ¼″ (6mm) seam allowance and leaving an opening for turning. Turn the brooch right side out, press it, and edgestitch it all the way around, closing the opening as you sew.

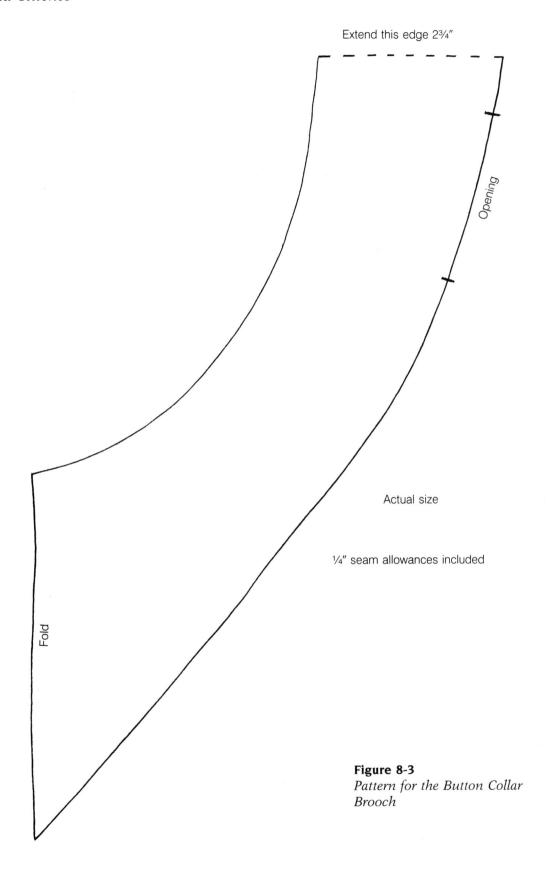

Extend this edge 2¾″

Opening

Fold

Actual size

¼″ seam allowances included

Figure 8-3
Pattern for the Button Collar Brooch

Stitch decorative buttons on the front of the brooch, starting in the center and working your way out to the edges. Put the larger, more interesting buttons in the center. As you get closer to the edges, use smaller, flatter buttons to allow the collar of the blouse to lie normally.

Sew a piece of closure tape to each end of the neckpiece. To wear the neckpiece, place the ends under the collar of the blouse and attach the closure tape together in the back. Pull the blouse collar out and over the edges of the brooch (Fig. 8-4).

This fanciful neckpiece can also be made without the buttons in an interesting fabric to add a touch of color or texture at the neckline.

Figure 8-4
The finished Collar Brooch is worn under the collar of a blouse.

▶ Button Cluster Pin (Fig. 8-5)

Pins made of clusters of interesting, unusual buttons have become quite popular in the last few years. Here's a technique for making them that will let you have beautiful jewelry while using up ordinary and not-so-interesting pieces. The gold pins shown in the Color Section were made from some button odds and ends that had been taking up space in my button box for years.

MATERIALS NEEDED

A small flat object to use as a base for the pin of the approximate size and shape that you want the finished pin (The base could be a piece of thick (at least ¼″ [6mm]), sturdy cardboard or a piece of wood or metal.)

Assorted buttons of almost any type, including plastic and discolored or faded ones

Glue gun

Spray paint or acrylic paint and a small brush

Pin back or barrette clip

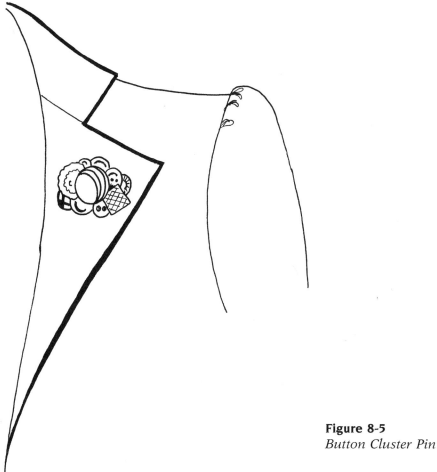

Figure 8-5
Button Cluster Pin

DIRECTIONS

Select the buttons for the pin. Choose a few that are textured or have a surface design. Using one dramatic color, paint each button separately. Turn the buttons over and paint the backs as well. Paint the base of the pin the same color as the buttons.

Arrange the buttons in a cluster, putting the ones with the most texture on the top. Glue the buttons in place with a glue gun.

Attach a pin back or a barrette clip to the back of the base.

Chapter 9
Creative Mending and Patching

Refurbishing Worn Clothing

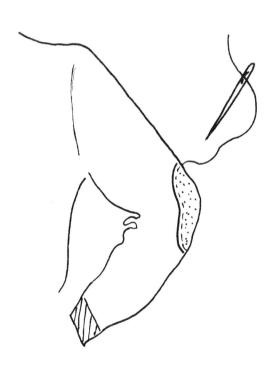

A FRIEND of mine once told me that she has the perfect system for mending. She keeps a basket near her sewing machine for the family clothes that are worn and torn. All the items that need to be mended go into the basket, and she leaves them there until they go out of style; then she throws them out. Most of us can relate to this method because the art of mending and patching clothing has all but vanished with our busy lifestyles. It is so much easier (and more fun!) to discard the worn garment and start with a new one. However, the garment will still be taking up space somewhere, whether it is in a landfill or in the back of your closet. Usually only a few minutes and a few pennies will make the garment at least serviceable and sometimes like new again. The next time you find a tear or stain, examine the piece of clothing and think about the possible ways you could refurbish and renew that garment.

With all of the new notions and fusibles on the market, mending actually has become easier even though we do it less. If you haven't tried your hand at a simple job of repairing a rip or tear, don't be afraid to experiment. What have you got to lose? You can't wear the garment with a hole in it, so you might as well use it to hone your mending skills.

▶ Tear Repairing

Repairing a rip or tear is probably the most common mending job we need to do. The kind of rips that happen usually fall into one of several categories: a split seam, a hole, or a three-corner tear. Follow these basic machine directions for taking care of each one.

MATERIALS NEEDED
Lightweight fusible interfacing
Darning thread (this is lightweight, usually 60 or 70 weight) to help avoid thread buildup as you stitch (Use the thread in both the needle and the bobbin and choose a color as close to the fabric as possible.)

DIRECTIONS
There are two methods of darning tears in fabrics. One uses the built-in stitches on your machine and is good for mending small straight tears or a three-corner rip. The other is a free-motion technique that allows you to move the fabric and cover a larger, open area. Repairing seams is easier than either of these techniques.

Small Tears

For a small straight tear or a three-corner rip, trim away any rough edges and loose threads. Fuse a small patch of lightweight interfacing behind the torn area, closing the tear as much as possible without puckering or pulling the fabric. If you don't want to use a fusible, substitute a piece of organdy and pin or baste it in place.

Use a medium zigzag stitch (or a running stitch if your machine has one) and sew several rows to cover the tear. Slightly overlap the parallel rows of stitching.

If the fabric is fairly lightweight, you may need to use some additional stabilizer behind your work to keep it from puckering. Use a pull-away stabilizer, such as Tear-away or Stitch & Tear. If in doubt, use the stabilizer. Pull it off the back of your work after you have repaired the tear.

Large Tears

For darning larger tears, use the free-motion technique. Trim the edges of the tear to remove any loose threads. Stretch the area in an embroidery hoop, placing the torn area in the center (Fig. 9-1). *Lower or cover the feed dogs on your sewing machine.* By doing this, your stitch length will not have any effect on the movement of the fabric and the fabric will move only if and where you move it.

Figure 9-1
Place the torn portion in an embroidery hoop.

Starting at the top left side of the tear, move the hoop with a smooth, continuous motion, working your way from the top of the tear to the bottom of the tear and creating a straight line of stitching. When you reach the bottom of the tear, slide the hoop slightly to the left and stitch back up to the top of the tear. Continue this up and down stitching until you've worked across the tear, ending with the needle in the fabric on the lower right side of the tear. Begin stitching in the same way as you just did, except this time work back and forth so that the stitching is at a right angle to the first stitches. Essentially, you are creating a patch made of thread.

As you move across the work, keep your hands on the hoop and move it at a consistent rate of speed to ensure even stitches. Don't try to fill in the tear too quickly; you want to build up the "thread patch" slowly and in layers so that the darned area will stay as soft and flat as possible. As you move the hoop, do so in smooth, round movements so that the stitches form curves rather than angles. Sharp edges may result in more strain on the tear and cause it to rip further.

Repeat these steps until you've completely covered the tear, being sure to fill in any spaces.

Split Seams

Repairing a split seam is a simple matter of pulling the fabric together and restitching on the previous seam line. For stress points, such as underarm or crotch areas, stitch a second time to reinforce them.

▶ Patching

DIRECTIONS

If the hole is simply too large to cover with thread, consider making a fabric patch. The fashion trends of the last few years have made it more acceptable—and even stylish!—to have visible patches on clothing. Patches can be applied in a number of ways. You can choose an inside patch, a reinforced patch, or a decorative patch.

If the area has worn thin but not completely through the fabric, try reinforcing it from the wrong side. The easiest way to do this is to use a fusible interfacing to reinforce the area behind the worn spot. You can add months to the life of a garment by doing this, especially for areas such as elbows and knees or other places that receive a great deal of friction and stress.

To make a visible patch on the outside of the garment, select a firm, tightly woven fabric. The weight should be as close to the weight of the garment fabric as possible. Avoid choosing a fabric so durable that it is too heavy for the garment. Cut the patch 1″ (2.5cm) larger than the hole on all sides and fuse a paper-backed fusible web to the back of it. Round the corners to get a better bond when applying the web to the worn area. Peel off the paper and position the patch over the hole. Fuse the patch to the garment and stitch around the edges using one of the four methods described below.

- Turn a scant ¼″ (6mm) under on all sides of the patch *before fusing it to the garment*. After fusing, edgestitch around all the edges to secure the patch (Fig. 9-2).

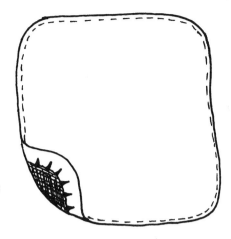

Figure 9-2
Turned-and-stitched edges

- After fusing the patch to the garment, use a medium-width satin stitch around all the edges, making sure to cover the raw edges completely (Fig. 9-3).

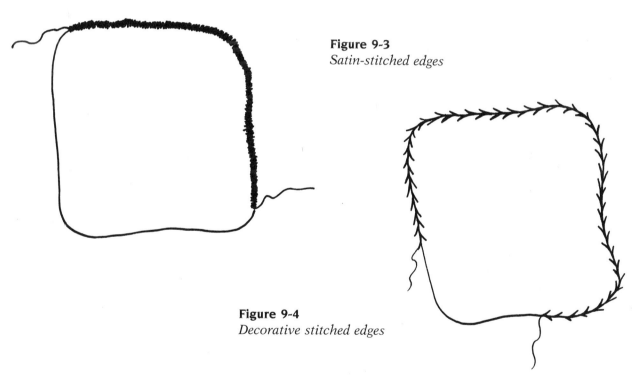

Figure 9-3
Satin-stitched edges

Figure 9-4
Decorative stitched edges

- After fusing, choose a decorative machine stitch and stitch around all the edges (Fig. 9-4). For good coverage and a durable edging, choose a stitch that moves from side to side.
- Cover the raw edge of the patch with bias tape before fusing it to the garment (Fig. 9-5). Use a straight stitch to secure the binding to the patch. Choose either a straight stitch or a decorative stitch to sew the patch onto the garment.

Figure 9-5
Bias-bound edges

A quilted patch (Fig. 9-6) will not only cover the hole but will last longer than a single-layer patch. Layer the patch fabric with a thin layer of fleece and a backing fabric if desired. Quilt with any design you want: Parallel lines, free-motion, stitched shapes. Bind the edges, place the patch over the hole, and edgestitch it in place.

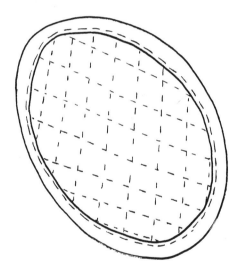

Figure 9-6
Quilted patch

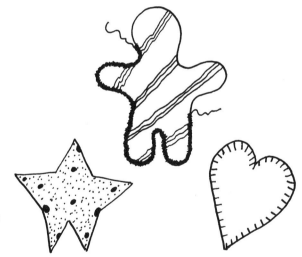

Figure 9-7
Decorative patch

In addition to being functional, patches can also be decorative. Choose a fun shape and incorporate it into the design of a garment. For example, make patches from cookie cutters (Fig. 9-7) or find illustrations and shapes in coloring books or magazines. After the patch fabric is cut into a decorative shape, back the patch with fusible web and apply it using one of the methods already described.

▶ **Stretched Edges** (Fig. 9-8)

DIRECTIONS

If you have sweaters, socks, or knit clothes that have stretched-out cuffs or hems, it's a simple matter to add more life to these garments. Restore those distorted or loose, stretched-out edges using elastic thread. Place one or two strands of elastic thread next to the edge and zigzag stitch over the thread and the edge, gently stretching the elastic as you stitch. The elastic thread will pull the edge in slightly and restore life to the garment.

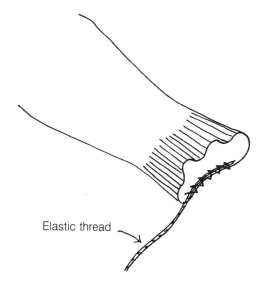

Figure 9-8
Restoring stretched edges on knit garments

Elastic thread

Chapter 10
Cleaning, Collecting, and Keeping

*Organizing and Storing
Recyclable Materials*

IN THE long run, recycling and reusing will reduce the amount of trash and throwaways going to the landfills. In the short run, you will begin to keep all kinds of things that might come in handy someday. This leads to the problem of what to do with all of this stuff. It would be easy to talk yourself out of recycling if you became buried in all the things you used to throw away.

With a little thought and organization, not only can you eliminate some of the clutter, but you'll know what you have and where to find it. When dealing with sewing supplies, my philosophy is, if I can see it, I will much more likely use it. It's easy to forget what you have and therefore never use it if it is neatly tucked away in a box or a closet. I try to keep as many things visible as possible. Open shelves are great for keeping things organized and in plain sight. Glass jars and recycled plastic bags also help in this effort.

The next best thing to having everything visible is to use labels. Boxes and bags are great to hold needed items, but be sure to label each one so you'll know what's inside without having to dig through them.

Most fabric stores throw away their cardboard fabric bolts and rolls. They can usually be yours for the asking. Roll any delicate fabrics that might crease from being folded and place the rolls in a basket or box. Label the ends of the rolls with the fiber content, width, and yardage, and whether or not the fabric is needle-ready.

Put fabric pieces of more than two yards onto a cardboard bolt and stack them neatly on a shelf or in a cabinet.

An old idea, but one that works every time, is to use discarded cereal and soap powder boxes to organize and store magazines and patterns. Mark the box as shown in Figure 10-1 and cut away the top part of the

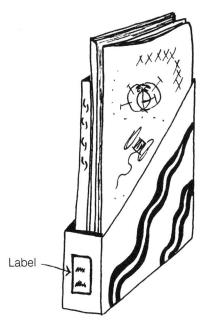

Label

Figure 10-1
Magazine Holder

box. You can use the box as is or paint it or cover it with fabric or adhesive-backed paper.

▶ Hanging See-Through Organizer (Fig. 10-2)

Make an easy hanging pocket bag to hold all sorts of odds and ends. The bag shown in the Color Section was designed by Charlou Lunsford, who teaches sewing methods and decorative machine techniques in the

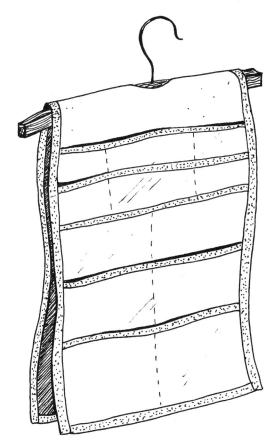

Figure 10-2
Hanging See-Through Organizer

Kansas City area. She uses this bag to store such treasures as special buttons or interesting thread so that when she's in the mood to experiment, she doesn't forget she has them. You can use this bag for any number of small items that you want to keep handy and in plain sight. The organizer slips over the top of a hanger and can be hung in the closet or on a wall. The finished size of the one shown is 14″ × 21¼″ (35.5cm × 54cm), but you can customize the size to fit your own needs.

MATERIALS NEEDED
2 rectangles, each 14″ × 22″ (35.5cm × 56cm), of canvas, denim, or
    other sturdy fabric

12 strips of medium-weight clear vinyl (can be part of a discarded shower curtain): 4 each 3″ × 14″ (7.5cm × 35.5cm), 4 each 4″ × 14″ (10cm × 35.5cm), and 4 each 5″ × 14″ (12.5cm × 35.5cm)

Bias strips for binding:

Outside edge—2½ yards (2.29m) of 2½″-wide (6.5cm) strips

Top edge of pockets—4½ yards (4.11m) of 1¼″-wide (3cm) strips

Bottom edge of pockets—3½ yards (3.20m) of 1″-wide (2.5cm) strips

DIRECTIONS

On the top 14″ (35.5cm) side of each canvas piece, find the center and measure out 2″ (5cm) on each side and mark.

Place two pieces of canvas right sides together and stitch from the mark out to the edges, using a ¾″ (2cm) seam allowance. Press the seam open all the way across the top edge. Turn under the raw edge of the seam allowances and edgestitch them.

You'll use the bias strips to cover the exposed edges of the vinyl pockets. First, fold the 1¼″ (3cm) binding strip in half lengthwise, wrong sides together, and press. Place the long raw edges of the folded strip even with one 14″ (35.5cm) edge of any pocket. Stitch, using a ⅛″ (3mm) seam allowance. Wrap the folded edge of the strip around to the back side of the vinyl and topstitch it in place. Repeat along the top edge of all the pockets.

Position the pocket strips across each side of the organizer, varying the order of the strips as you desire and making sure the pocket tops on each side face toward the top center hole of the organizer. Stitch each pocket in place across its bottom edge. Cover this exposed bottom edge of vinyl using the 1″ (2.5cm) strips of bias. Fold under ¼″ (6mm) on each long side of the bias strip and press. Lay the strip over the lower edge of the pocket and topstitch along each folded edge of the strip. Repeat this step for each pocket, except the ones at the lower edges.

Cut two 14″ (35.5cm) pieces of the 2½″ (6.5cm) bias strips. Fold each in half lengthwise, wrong sides together, and press. Place the folded strip across the lower edge of the organizer with all raw edges even and stitch through all layers, using a ¼″ (6mm) seam allowance. Wrap the folded edge of the strip around to the back side of the vinyl and topstitch it in place. Repeat this procedure along the sides, making sure to fold in the ends of the bias at the lower edge before topstitching.

Slip the organizer over a hanger and hang it in your closet or on the wall.

Whether you're planning to recycle old clothes and nylons, extra fabric, or hardware from handbags and belts, take the time to devise a storage system that keeps everything as neat and as visible as possible. You'll be much more likely to recycle if you do.

Afterword
A Way of Life

"USE IT UP, wear it out, make it do, or do without." This old Yankee proverb was a way of life in earlier times, and because of it, waste and misuse were the exception, rather than the rule. We would be wise to heed this today, not only to control the amount of garbage and trash, but also to extend our resources and make them stretch as far as possible.

I'd like this book to do more than inspire you to sew; I'm hoping it also encourages you to see the world around you in a new way.

Once you begin to look for recycling possibilities in your sewing room, you will find it easy to integrate the process into your daily life. It takes only a small effort to start the ball rolling and make a difference in the fight to save the earth. Passing this way of thinking along to your children, friends, co-workers, and associates will help spread the attitudes and actions that we need to perpetuate the recycling effort.

Glossary

Closure tape—Hook-and-loop closure, such as Velcro, that can be used in place of buttons, hooks, or zippers.

Couching—A technique consisting of stitching over cord.

Edgestitch—Straight stitching close to edge. Usually done on a folded or finished edge.

Entredeux—A narrow strip of batiste with a row of decorative holes on it that look similar to hemstitching. In heirloom sewing, traditionally placed between lace and fabric for strength and beauty.

Fusible web—Bonding material used to fuse two pieces of fabric together. Sometimes has a paper backing that peels away.

Needle-ready—Refers to fabric that has been dry cleaned or prewashed and is ready for sewing.

Satin stitch—A zigzag stitch with a narrow stitch length that produces a heavy filled-in look.

Stabilizer—Material used to add body and stability to a piece of fabric. Varieties include interfacing, pull-away stabilizer, and water-soluble stabilizer.

Recommended Reading

101 Ways to Save Money and Save Our Planet by the Green Group (New Orleans: Paper Chase Press, 1992).

The First Green Christmas by The Evergreen Alliance (San Francisco: Halo Books, 1990).

The Green Consumer by John Elkington, Julia Hailes, and Joel Makower (New York: Tilden Press, 1988).

New Clothes from Old by Gloria R. Mosesson (Indianapolis: Bobbs-Merrill, 1977).

The Recyclers Handbook by The Earth Works Group (Schenevus, New York: Greenleaf, 1990).

Short Kutz by Melanie Graham (Radnor, PA: Chilton, 1991).

List of Recycled Items

The following index lists supplies and materials used in the projects in this book. It is intended to help you save and use these items rather than throw them out. So, if you're cleaning out a closet or wondering what to do with the supplies left over from a just-finished sewing project, consult this list for ideas. Perusing the list may even provide you with the inspiration to start a recycling project . . . sooner, rather than later.

Index